The Roads
to Nowhere

A Child of Lebanon

Father Mansour Labaky

Translated by Annelyse M. Allen

ST. BEDE'S PUBLICATIONS
Petersham, Massachusetts

Cover design: Bernadette Jaeger, OSB
Cover photo by Wide World Photos

LIBRARY OF CONGRESS CATALOGING IN PUBLICATION DATA

Labaky, Mansour.
  The roads to nowhere.

  Translation of: L'enfant du Liban.
  1. Lebanon—History—1975-   —Fiction. I. Title.
PQ3979.2.L3E513   1987   843   87-32305
ISBN 0-932506-61-5

Published by St. Bede's Publications
     P.O. Box 545
     Petersham, MA 01366-0545

1

When I was a child, I could see the sea from my mountain. There it lay, all the way to the far end of the West—beautiful, immense, mysterious. Its summer mornings were like blue silk, its noons were splashed with light, and its clear nights dazzled with the stars and moon.

I believed the horizon was its limit, where the sun would snuggle down in a shimmer of purple and gold or sometimes sink into a heap of clouds—a sure sign that rain was soon to come.

At the foot of my mountain, the sea washed a thin strip of coast which stretched into long orchards of citrus trees. When they blossomed, the breeze carried their fragrance up the mountainside. Actually, we were much too high up to ever get a whiff of the perfumes of the plain, but if my mother could smell them with a gleam of happy emotion in her eyes, could I not smell them too? So I sniffed with conviction, imitating her in her perceptions, never minding my own.

My mother was my mother and I firmly believed she could hear, smell and see a whole lot of things that were not accessible to others. For instance, when on summer nights we savored the splendors of the star-studded sky, I was convinced she could actually see through into the paradise she was telling me of. As I cuddled against her, it was the softness in her voice, much more than her words, which filled me with the mysterious, yet so intense, presence of God.

I later found out that among my mother's happiest memories was the fragrance of orange blossoms. I understood, much later still, that one could actually "smell" with one's memory.

Green and chestnut brown in all seasons, our semblance
of a shore was speckled with white here and there on the
capes where houses huddled, like so many herds of sheep,
to form towns.

Immediately beyond the orchards rose the mountains,
undulating far away to the South and further still to the
North. But in the East, I could only see the woody curve of
the hill that hung over our village and I believed that there
lay the end of the earth.

*   *   *

One day, my Jeddo* perched me on his shoulders and we
climbed together to the top of the hill. To my surprise, I
discovered valleys and yet more mountains, all the more
impressive a sight because there was no sea to limit them. I
looked at them for a long time as I slowly came to understand that beyond what our eyes can see are other worlds
still, worlds that seem to reach the sky if they are not, quite
simply, without end. Where, then, did the earth end?

"What's all that?" I asked my Jeddo.

"All that is our country," he replied, laughing at my
surprise. "All that is Lebanon."

"But on the sea side, it's all our village, isn't it?" I asked.

"No," said Jeddo, "it's also Lebanon. Our village is only
where our own houses are, yours and those of the people
you know well and see every day. Our village is only a tiny
bit of our country."

"And those houses there, and there, and up there and
down there," I asked, pointing in every direction, "they're
not our village, then?"

"No," said Jeddo, "they are other villages. Each one has
its own name and they are all in Lebanon."

"And the sea, is it also our country?"

---

*Grandfather

"No," said Jeddo, "only a small part of it is, near the coast. The sea takes you to other countries and other seas. And beyond our mountains are more countries and more seas."

"Ah!" I said, dazzled by the size and diversity of a world that I was just beginning to perceive. "Ah! Our village is not the whole earth, then?"

"No," said Jeddo, "but our village in our country is all the land we have."

"And after the other countries and the other seas, what is there? Is it where the sky begins? Where does the earth end? Can we see another country from here? Do..."

I asked a thousand questions and Jeddo explained to me so many wonders that I ended up mixing the sky and the earth together.

But that evening, at bedtime, I felt my village was around me like my mother's arms. It was no longer a vague entity floating between the horizon and the top of our mountains—until then, the boundaries of my world. It now seemed to have shrunk as my universe became immense, but in the process, it had taken shape and body.

I was only a small boy among so many others and it was only a small village among so many others. But like me it had a name; like me it had its own place in the universe; like me it was loved; like me it was alive.

That is what my Jeddo breathed into me up there, on the hill, as he taught me that the horizon is not the end of anything but always the beginning of "elsewhere."

*   *   *

Later, I came to take my village somewhat for granted. I would look at it without really seeing it, the way one would pass by objects which have become so familiar that one only remembers them when they are no longer around. It was there, and so was I. But while my village did not change, the horizon began to drift towards me in a confused medley of reality and fiction, of sweetness and violence, of beauty and ugliness very different from what we experienced at home.

Ah, the compelling power of television! I was still too young to appreciate the singers who contorted themselves to music that buzzed like a swarm of giant bees, or the endless series of drama. The plots of the thrillers completely escaped me and all I remembered was that everyone in them seemed to be constantly chasing everyone else and shooting completely at random. It made me shiver, but more from fear than from excitement, although these images seemed to remain somehow outside my consciousness. They did not affect my real life and fed neither my dreams nor my games, even though I sometimes fancied myself as a rocket-man with my legs two fire-spitting fins and my nose a propeller that hummed at supersonic speed through a yellow sky streaked with red and black.

I was a child of the mountain, blessed with enough space, splendid landscapes and, most of all, gentle peacefulness to become naturally open to the beauty of things. Much more fascinating than the cacophony of television was the blue, silent, faraway stillness of the sea where I fancied myself rolling and gliding forever. Or the moving, gold-specked shadows of our mulberry tree. Or the honey which poured from the honeycomb: how could that possibly be the work of such tiny bugs? Or, among other things, our pet turtle's oddities.

I still haven't found out whether all turtles in the world share the same intriguing peculiarity. When cold weather drew near (I can't remember whether it was at the first October rains or a little later, towards mid-autumn), our turtle would give up the garden's plentiful delights and take up the life of a recluse inside the house where she hibernated until spring near the living room stove. Even more surprising, she would stubbornly refuse any food. Whenever the sun broke through the clouds, I sometimes tried to take my recluse outdoors for a breath of fresh air, but no sooner had she smelled the soil than she would hurry back to her spot by the stove and let me know how annoyed she was by withdrawing her head inside her shell. This hurt my feelings considerably, since she usually swung her head contentedly when I spoke to her.

On March 21, not a day before or after—Allah be my witness!—our turtle migrated back to the garden. If she ran into a closed door on her way out, she would prop herself against it and scratch it with her front paws until finally one of us would take it upon himself to let her out.

"Why is she going out today?" I once asked Yussef, my eldest brother.

"Because it is March 21."

"So, what's so special about it?"

"It's the first day of spring."

"How does she know it?"

"Why do trees blossom in the spring? How do they know it's spring? Because of the new mildness in the air and a thousand other signs. Well, I assume it's the same thing for your turtle. She *knows* and *feels* it, that's all."

"Yes, but trees blossom for weeks and weeks and not all of them at the same time. They don't wait for a set date. Why does she come out today and not yesterday or the day before, or tomorrow, or the day after?"

"There is a simple way to find out," Yussef teased me. "Why don't you go and ask her? Who knows, she might tell you!"

A few days later, I remembered that my cousin Milad also had a turtle and I ran to his house to find out about her habits. I found him sprawled near a rosebush in deep meditation in front of a caterpillar whose superbly green body seemed to be embossed with equally sumptuous blue beads. I promptly forgot the purpose of my visit and fell to his side.

"Oh!" I whispered, rendered practically voiceless by the

sight of such beauty. "Can you lend her to me until tomorrow?"

"I wish I could," he sighed, "but I can't even lend her to myself."

"Why? Last year, I let you have all my beetles."

"Yes, yes, but I won't borrow them anymore. This, and the beetles, they are meant to live outside. They're meant to be free."

"Who told you?"

"My papa."

"What is it, to be free?"

"I don't know. It's the opposite of being locked up like when we stick them into matchboxes."

"Does living outdoors mean being free?"

"I don't know. What I do know is I would have liked to take her everywhere with me and even lend her to you a little. She is so beautiful!"

That, the caterpillar was. Regally so. But, as we say at home, "Oh novelty, you are beautiful for being new. Oh old things, your time is passed."

The very next day, I was ecstatically leafing through the first book of tales I had ever been given to read. Lamia, the elder of my two sisters, had given it to me for my sixth birthday. Its title sounded like the Milky Way that would lead to wonders beyond the star-filled sky. Just think—*One Thousand and One Nights*! Could that mean anything but the eternity of Heaven itself suddenly revealed as one thousand and one Christmas nights with one thousand and one seraphim fluttering around and one thousand and one mangers wreathed in a garland of one thousand and one stars?

"Is this the story of the paradise which never ends and of its beginning?" I asked with the hope of finally discovering the *before* of all things. For if I took eternity for granted, as I did the present and future (the world, now or ever, without me and my family was simply inconceivable), I found it hard to accept that there was not a starting point, a beginning a *before* God and His creation.

"Oh, no!" cried Lamia. "It's not *that* at all. It's Sinbad, Aladdin and company. You're not going to be disappointed, I hope?"

It was not *that* at all, indeed. It was something else altogether—a fabulous world which abolished the boundaries of the visible and invisible, of the possible and impossible more assuredly than did the top of our hill. That day, I crossed rockets off my imaginary travels. No more flames for taking off, no more blasts to land on the moon, no more swarms of giant bees for music. Endlessly dazzling images, flutes, lutes, tambourines, magic rings and lamps, gold-domed cities, gardens, perfumes, fairy-tale colors. . . . This magic universe was crowded with thieves and cheaters, people who were by nature jealous, malevolent and driven by their ambition but ended up sooner or later defeated precisely by their own vileness and the constant miraculous triumph of innocent hearts. In a word, it was fantastic.

With a turban on my head and "babouche" slippers on my feet, I felt lighter than a leaf in the wind when I opened my book and took off on a flying carpet which carried me to the seventh heaven "beyond the seventh sea and the ninth mountain."

My village too was fantastic. It filled me so completely with beauty and certainty that clouds became marvelously accessible. I imagined them circling around the earth and I told myself that tomorrow, when I grew up, I would leave for far away places, wherever any road could take me. And each time, I would come back to my village, for the thought of leaving it forever had never entered my mind.

*   *   *

At any rate, in those days, words like *never* or *war* did not make any sense at all, cozily perched as I was at the edge of the world and living a blessed *forever* that included a *today* radiant with love and a *tomorrow* more promising and singing than a fountain in the Spring.

I did not know then that war was about to blow away my sky and that the first path offered to my dreams of horizons would be a black, oppressing one-way tunnel where my heart would one day beat from sheer terror instead of love. Nor did I know that my village had already set the cadence of my steps and shaped the nuances of my outlook on the world and the intensity of my welcome to the song of life.

"At home, in our village," people around me used to say. "At home, in our village," recall the Lebanese throughout the world. And our foreign friends wonder: Why is it that the Lebanese say "At home, in our village!" with such a look of bliss on their faces that it seems what they really mean is, "At home, in paradise"?

Oh, foreign brother, where did you take root? Which place on earth is murmuring inside you like the rising sap in the tree?

Oh, foreign brother, I, like you, can see, because there is a place on earth which has offered me reality as a foretaste of eternity.

I can hear because there is a place on earth which has the voice of my father, and that of my mother.

I love, and I know I am alive because there is a place on earth which has kneaded me with faith and love.

This place on earth, this "at home, in the village" is my father. It is my mother. It is my Jeddo and my Teta* and the lives of all the villagers before and after me which are spread out in the vast and deep forest that reaches up to the stars. It is my house, all the more vibrant because it was mingled with other houses.

It is my first prayer as a little child sitting on my mother's

---

*Grandmother

lap with her hands joining mine. It is the bells of our small church tinkling like a bluebell in the soft breeze.

It is the curves of our orchards like so many horizons, and any and all of the people and things which opened up my heart to all other hearts.

And when my heart was closed for a long time because of the war and sank into the oblivion of life itself, this "at home, in my village" patiently set out to brighten it up anew. It came as a mixture of things past, and imposed itself in a language full of imagery, with the rhythmic whimsy of memories. It imposed itself as a simple adherence to life.

It revived in my heart a long-forgotten taste for a world where the slightest thing had an important and specific meaning. In that world each name was a whole story, and time knew no dates and was only measured by the pace of the seasons and the joys and trials of the peasants.

And, most of all, it enabled my heart to communicate with Jad, a little boy from another devastated village who spoke the same language, was born to the same enchanting landscapes, bathed in the same spring of love and enamoured of the same sweetness and peace.

2

As long as I live, war will remain for me the incarnation of hell. It taught me death when I was just becoming aware of my own existence.

It taught me the unfathomable depth of "never again" while, until then, my family's presence had seemed eternal as love itself.

It robbed me of my village, my house, my family.

It threw me and so many others out on roads that led to nowhere, far away from what had been home, aching in the silence for the security of a familiar face and for gestures and words of tenderness. It left us instead with the coldness of brutal deprivation and memories riddled with sufferings, which we could share only with strange and unfamiliar traveling companions.

I had no idea a village could be so fragile. I did not know that houses and people could be knocked down as easily as ninepins. My mother had not told me those things, she who told me of paradise and stars.

Her cold, limp hand in the midst of all the rubble. Her hand suddenly mute and foreign in my little hand.

Her dead hand.

I screamed. I implored her to please be warm again. To please give me some of her warmth again. I looked around me. Where was my house? Where was my father? Where were Yussef, Lamia, Milad and Hala, my brothers and sisters? Where were my Jeddo and my Teta? Had they too sunk into the silence of death? Why did they not answer me, they whose voices alone made tenderness palpable to me? Why did they leave me alone—me, the youngest, me their little one? I could not live without them. They were my life, my breath, my present and my forever. Why did they leave me alone?

Alone!

Their silence engulfed me like a tide of death. And I howled. I howled until my whole being became enclosed inside my mother's frozen hand...until my voice finally blended into her silence.

*   *   *

Before I knew it, I found myself in an orphanage. How did I get there? Who brought me? I don't remember. I only remember the huge door closing on two grey silhouettes.

Anyway, it was drizzling and everything was grey: the sky, the big house where I had just been brought, the nuns' veil-framed faces and their unfamiliar voices, the silent door-lined hallways, my fear, my overwhelming sense of exile.

I heard something like an infinitely sad wail. Was it the door or my own heart creaking?

Motionless, I stared at the two grey door panels.

Motionless, it seemed, forever.

I no longer had a body or a soul for I didn't feel a link to anything alive.

On the other side of that door was...my life. On this side, I only felt the emptiness of a nowhere which resembled the grey thump of bells tolling in the fog.

Why bother to move?

To walk is to go towards someone or something.

To look is to recognize someone or something.

To listen is to hear or wait for someone or something.

To laugh, to run, to sing, to play, to pray and to rough-house...and to cry in a burst of certainty: "Mama, I love you, do you love me?"

Mama!

From now on I could only love you in despair and that was worse than the darkest of nights.

Someone must have talked to me. Someone must have kissed me. I don't remember. I was too cold. And too hurt.

I was led through an empty corridor. A door opened into an empty room where the silence was too reminiscent of my village after its destruction—the forsaken silence of a bottomless abyss. A silence devoid of thought, devoid of promise. I felt I was stepping into nothingness.

Another door was opened into another corridor which led to a courtyard. The noise exploded in my ears. Never had I seen so many children playing in such a small space.

*　　*　　*

At home, the schoolyard opened into the woods. When it rained, we just slipped on our parkas with hoods flying in the wind and charged ahead in the downpour. The children of the mountains are a sturdy lot. They are immune to bad weather. Perched on a rock, we would play "Noah's Ark." We were giraffes, lions or dinosaurs, and whoever happened to be Noah hoisted his make-believe gangplank as we swung all together to simulate the surf. We had hundreds of games for rainy days and when the thunder rumbled, we knew we must keep clear of the shelter of the trees for fear of being struck by lightning.

But which of us would have cared for shelter anyway? The water which poured from the clouds was too good and it was such a treat to lift up our faces and drink from the very sky. For some reason, it gave us a feeling of freedom and of weightlessness which even beat running in the sun.

Ah! To swirl in the storm, to be the giant grass and bend in the wind. To be the boat, pitching in the white waves. To be the foam, to be the flame, to be the rainbow and write oneself in the colors of alliance between the storm and its clear aftermath. To be the whispering brook that winds around the pine trees towards the path to the village, and towards the sparkling fire waiting at home and Mama's feigned indignation: "Does my heart consider himself wet enough to finally deign to come in? I am going to let you drip on the porch like an umbrella."

Ah! to be an umbrella, to spread and flap one's arms open and closed, to shake the rain, flap, flap. "Mama, feel me, see, I'm almost dry. Please, couldn't you put me inside on the rack?"

And Mama's laughter, light, so light and tender, so tender that one forgot to play and threw oneself into her arms dripping with rain and happiness.

The way we were yesterday—present...and alive!

*   *   *

Someone called in a very loud voice which rose above the uproar: "Jad, Jad, here is Naseem, come quick to welcome him!"

In the confused swarm of children who were racing back and forth I spotted a little boy who hastened towards us with a smile.

"Good evening, Naseem," he said. He hesitated a long while before adding in a whisper: "If you want, we'll be friends. I know you've lost your voice, but who cares? There are other ways to talk, you'll see."

Who cared, indeed? I had lost much more than my voice. I had lost *everything* including the magic of the rain, and the voice of this little stranger with his wide, dark eyes reached me as in a dream.

O Jad, why bother to speak, if my family can't hear me? Why bother to speak if I can't hear my family?

Jad pulled me by the hand. I followed him passively. Going one way or the other, forward or backward, what difference could it make from now on? My steps were not mine anymore: they had lost the way to my home.

The orphanage. A gigantic cage in the hollowest part of a valley. Had I not been drowned in my family's absence, could I ever have grown accustomed to this incredibly square, compartmentalized and orderly world? There was nothing, absolutely nothing that looked like home, not even the tidiness which was as stiff and odorless as a whitewashed wall.

The first nights, I sniffed the sheets, hoping for a familiar smell. How rapturously I would have breathed in the sweet fragrance of lavender, full of sunshine and of the buzz of bees. With my mother and my sisters, we would pick it by the armful and shell it like ears of wheat into large wicker trays. Mama then refilled the sachets she hid in the cupboards so that we could breathe in the summer in the heart of winter.

I was assigned a place in the dormitory, a place in the dining hall, a place in class, a place in the study hall, a place in chapel. I assigned myself a place in a corner of the schoolyard, on a stone bench, always the same.

I was given new clothes. I wore a pair of pants and a shirt which had not been picked, washed or pressed by Mama. Nothing was left of home. Thus came to pass the ultimate break from my family.

Images flashed in my mind of my mother with her mending basket. She would pick up a sock and exclaim: "Allah, how expert my little ones are at making huge holes. Insh'Allah* that every child may be preserved to his parents!"

She stuck her needle in and out, mending everything perfectly and—how could I ever forget it!—she would lay a kiss on each mended sock before putting it away.

Such was my mother: a spring of happiness for everyone around her. She did not clothe us in garments only. She clothed us with her gaze, with the softness of her voice and of her demeanor, with the kisses she would nestle in her baskets and the lavender in her linen closets.

She said to us: "How beautiful and good are you, the

---

*God willing.

basil in my garden! Come near me that I may taste you a bit!"

And my father laughed: "Ya Mara,* when you're through with feasting on your children, maybe you can tell me where you put my coat?"

Oh my mother, what have I become now for the others? It was by your tender love that I was made good and handsome. At the orphanage, I could be no one's "sprig of basil." I was only a big boy, old enough to be on his own.

A big boy of seven, Mama, one does not take him in one's lap. One talks to him rationally. One loves him reasonably. That's only logical. After all, hasn't he reached the age of reason?

The "age of reason," Mama, does it have to be the end of the age of tenderness? Just the way baby teeth finally all fall out?

   * * *

For a while, in the beginning, I lived in a strange state of dissociation. Nothing and no one seemed real, neither me, nor the others. Stupefied and docile, I entered a daily routine which the orphanage bell mechanically sliced up with dull regularity.

It rang and we walked in single file from the dorm to the corridors, from the corridors to the dining hall, from the dining hall to the classroom.

It rang and we shut our grammar books and spread out our arithmetic cards.

It rang and the Sisters who seemed to be forever running after something—was it after time?—clapped their hands: "Let's hurry up children, hurry up!"

It rang and I was startled by its shrill stiffness. I know things are the same in every school. But there, that detest-

---

*Oh, wife.

able bell kept us trotting from morning till night. There was no way to escape it even after school hours. It was all reminders and summonses. Couldn't it, at least when we went to chapel, sound like the call of our bell back home— light, flexible and free as a flying swallow?

What was the hurry, anyway, hour after hour, day after day, month after month? To whom were we running?

Could I ever have grown used to the Sisters? I don't know. I did not see them. It was not only that pain made me blind to any new face, but, between them and me, between the others and me, death had dug such large and empty spaces that any kind of communication was impossible for me. I could only perceive shadows and I did not even wonder what we were all doing there, in this closed environment where life seemed to run around in circles to the abominable hammering of a bell.

Sometimes, I still thought to myself: "Tomorrow, when I grow up..."

I just repeated it to say something, something that would be totally different from "today." But my thought had no resonance because "tomorrow" seemed as grey and mute as a Fall mist. I could no longer make myself imagine that some day I would really be grown up and that I could then alter the course of my life.

I felt as if time had stopped on my orphan's distress and condemned me to remain forever a child, forever silent and docile, with my heart and throat forever in a tight knot.

Yet I did not cry. Never in the daytime. Never in front of the many searching looks which probed my silence. Their numbers frightened me and what could I have told them? I waited for the night, when they were asleep, to go back to my family, out there at home, in the village where once upon a time all the light in the world used to be concentrated because their love was in me and around me and nourished me with happiness.

But at night, I was afraid of the darkness and of the

invisible presence which I felt prowling around my bed. My imagination threw me in a panic and I thought I could see the devil, war and death: three strangely identical skeletons, black as the hell from where they had surely come. They stared at me with a sneer that was all the more sinister because I could not hear it. I shook with terror under my blankets. I choked back a sob as I called my mother. I knew she would never again answer me. But I also knew, without being able to put it into words, that from now on she only lived in me and through me who called her at every second, and I kept hold of her with all the strength of my sorrow for that was now my only link to life.

3

Jad, it is to you and for you that I am writing, because after my family's death, you alone have loved me with a mother's heart.

Yes, Jad, with a mother's heart.

And yet, you were only seven. Like me. And you were an orphan. Like me.

Only you still had your father, a wounded, penniless refugee without a job. But alive!

He was your hope. You knew he would take you out as soon as he recovered. Together, you dreamed, you would find a room and some work. You were only passing by, drawing your vitality and happiness from the future, whereas I was stagnating in my dead past.

You were sweet and swift as a squirrel.

And you talked so much. Allah, how talkative you were!

You said to me later: "I had to speak for two!" You did not add, "And to love for two. And to live for two." Yet that was just what you did and this is why I can say that you have loved me with a mother's heart.

When a little boy gets up at night because another little boy cries, when he wraps his arms around him and simply says: 'Cry, Naseem, but I am going to make you smile, because. . . . Oh! if only I could be your mother for a single second, at least when you are crying!' —at seven, Jad, I call this the height of understanding, of sharing, of love.

And you smiled, Jad. With tears in your eyes and in your voice, but you smiled. Bravely, warmly, wonderfully.

At school, at mealtime, at chapel, I was placed next to you. In the dorm, you were in the bed next to mine, to my right. To my left was the wall, so I could turn away from you without having to meet someone else's gaze.

But who could have stopped your babbling away? On a desert island, you would have talked to the waves, to the clouds, to the wind, to yourself. Was it to counterbalance my muteness that the nuns had placed us side by side? Or was it because of your sweet kindness, so obvious, so genuine that only it could break into my silence?

*   *   *

My first night at the orphanage was terrible. Far away at the other end of the dorm, just above the door, the night light was only a tiny spot, much too pale to dissipate the darkness. The beds, covered with ash-colored blankets, were lined up in three rows which looked to me like so many tombstones and, in my panic, I became convinced that I was sleeping in a graveyard. My teeth were chattering so much that I felt I was going to wake up all those dead, whose deep and loud breathing should have been enough to reassure me.

Jad, had you also experienced the hallucinations of a first solitary night in this strange place peopled by strange shadows? You got out of your bed with infinite precautions. Your deliberately slow movements, coupled with your oversized pajamas whose drooping sleeves swayed back and forth in the dark, made you look like a ghost. You raised your arms to wave at me. That was too much. I would have screamed had I still had my voice. I ducked a bit further under my covers, pressing myself into the mattress with all my weight, in the hope that I would manage to sink into it, convinced as I was that you were about to snatch me and turn me into another ghost.

Had I known one could kill oneself, I would have jumped out of the window. To break free from you. To run away from this graveyard and my unbearable feeling of loneliness. To abolish my terror. To be reunited with my family anywhere, be it in another graveyard, as long as I was with them. Among them. Surrounded by them.

The icy cold hand of my mother was better than this haunted place. By the time I had finally been pried away from Mama's hand, it had no longer seemed cold, as I, myself, had become as a stone—as cold as she was. But still with her.

Her broken body, her burnt face had become my body and my face. This was the way I perceived myself that first night: ripped apart, bloody, totally given away to death, while you were waving your sleeves above my bed.

But I did not know that one could kill oneself. No one had ever mentioned suicide in my presence, I could only shiver and call to the broken image of my mother.

Then I heard your voice at last: "Listen to me, Naseem, please listen! I can't speak any louder. Sister Marie would come running in. She always comes to see the newcomers before she goes to bed anyway. You're scared? Me too. I'm always scared at night. And I cried, Oh, St. Elijah, how I used to cry in the beginning! And I called Mama. Oh, St. Elijah, how I called her! Listen, Naseem: the faster you go to sleep, the less long you'll shake. Say a prayer. My Mama used to say...she used to say...."

I never heard what your mother used to say to ward off the terrible visions of a war orphan. Sister Marie appeared at the end of the dorm and, quicker than a mouse, you slipped back between your sheets. She was still quite far away and you were already fast asleep, with that talent you still have for falling abruptly asleep in the middle of a sentence, of a gesture, sometimes of a laugh.

As for me, I closed my eyes, lonely and miserable as ever. No prayer came back to my death-beleaguered memory. I tried, though. Sister Marie's hand lightly stroked my hair. I did not stir. She went on with her rounds and I could hear her rosary beads clinking along. A prayer? My lips mechanically began: "Hail, Ma..." "Ma..." as in Mama! My broken Mama. My broken family. I tried to stop thinking about it, but the bombs kept exploding in my head. I saw

again house walls tottering before they crashed down
...and, more intolerable than anything else, my family's
bodies bathed in their own blood.

I let myself sink into delirium, reciting until exhaustion
finally put me to sleep: "Hail, Mama, dead, dead, forever
and ever...."

*   *   *

The orphanage swarmed with orphans, of course. And
with social cases.

The first time Ramzi, an unruly and quarrelsome little
boy, planted himself in front of me and blurted out superbly: "I am a Soshalcase!" (that's what it sounded like), "and
you, what are you?" I was nonplussed, believing he must
be some sultan of a kind unknown in the *One Thousand and
One Nights*.

Having to suffer its consequences myself, I knew that
war could be the source of many upsets. Why wouldn't a
prince's son find himself suddenly confined with ordinary
children? I stared at Ramzi with undisguised curiosity and
was rather disappointed to see that he looked in no way
different from anyone else.

I could not tell him: "Me? I am a peasant's son," since I
still couldn't speak. Jad came to my rescue and announced
emphatically: "He is a *double* orphan."

Double! Oh, St. George, how sharp and final this
sounded in the ensuing silence.

"Ah," Ramzi finally said, visibly annoyed at finding himself without a reply.

"Ah!" My mouth formed the word, but no sound came
out. I simply felt as if I'd been punched in the stomach.

Mistaken by my expression, Jad hurried to explain:
"Social cases are children whose parents have problems."

That did not help me much. I was aware that all adults
have some problem or other—more or less serious, more
or less complicated. At home, people tried to unravel them

together, sometimes further entangling them when opinions varied from one extreme to the other. But, in the end, everyone finally ended up being reasonable, and things went back to their normal daily course. Apart from death and incurable illnesses (we had not experienced war yet), everything could be fixed—material losses as well as quarrels and frustrated hopes. As far as I knew, no one had ever been given an elaborate name like "social case," and no child had ever been separated from his parents because of problems.

At first, I envied the "Soshalcase" represented by Ramzi. With or without problems, this lucky duck still had his parents. I could not understand his defiant looks and his never-ending revolt, when he should have been rejoicing, dancing with joy. One day, his parents would come to get him, like the father whose tenderness Jad was constantly singing.

Jad avoided Ramzi (his "tiresome right hand side neighbor" as he called him), because everything in him reeked of violence. He was too fond of noise, provocations and fights, and, besides, he was very stubborn.

I can still picture him shouting to Sister Marie (I can't remember why), "Leave me alone! You're not my mother! I don't need you or anyone else!"

Not anyone, Ramzi? One night, we heard you calling your mother. Your delirious childish cry chilled our hearts. Jad, who had been quietly chatting, turned towards you, determined to ignore any rebuff. But you were asleep. You were imploring in your sleep, and Jad whispered to me: "It's funny, don't you think? When someone asks him where his parents live, he answers that it's nobody's business, or that they are sick, or that they are preparing a wonderful house with a room full of toys. He says that when he goes away with them, he will do what he wants from morning till night. You know what? He lies. He lies because they have problems and he does not know if he'll ever be able to be with them. And you know what else? I'm scared of him because he can think of nothing but hitting people. My Mama did not like that. She used to say that those who hit—sometimes, they need our help because they're unhappy. But Ramzi, he won't listen to anybody. If he was awake, he would have shouted at me to leave him alone."

Jad did not speak for a long while, and I thought he was asleep. But suddenly he rose on his elbow and said something astonishing for a seven year-old: "You know what else? It's like he doesn't want to be loved, and it's not easy to help someone who doesn't want to be loved."

I would have liked to be able to ask Jad if people who made war were unhappy people who refused to be loved. But, no! War was too horrible. Only monsters could kill like that and destroy everything.

I realize now that in spite of Jad's very shrewd "You know what's," we were far from grasping the depth of Ramzi's distress.

To have parents and not to be able to live with them because they have problems...to feel rejected and abandoned, and to tell oneself stories which deny the obvious... to build one's future in sand castles which one knows very well are bound to be destroyed by the waves of those "problems"...to long for what has never existed and may never exist...all this is too much of a burden. It is such a burden that one defiantly, even proudly, for fear of bursting with pain, sums it up in a cry: "I am a Soshalcase!"

Oh, Ramzi, Jad and I were too young to understand your "problem," otherwise, we would have come by your side together, in spite of you, to make you feel less cold.

But who can fill the vacuum created by such neglect? I could at least dream of my past, and Jad could embellish his with a tomorrow brimming with plans. I had been loved; he still was loved. That was undisputedly ours. We did not need to tell ourselves stories to make up for what had never existed.

Oh, Ramzi, you were the one who loved in absolute despair. But I did not know it.

Today, Jad and I think of you with sadness, and tenderness: this word which used to make you sneer. We hope that somewhere on your path you found this tenderness for the lack of which you could not love your own self or believe in our friendship.

Apart from Jad and, inevitably, Ramzi, whose outbursts were deliberately theatrical, I still was not looking at anyone.

Soon, Jad became my private and public spokesman. I don't know by what blessed intuition he was able to decipher me with such ease. I think it must be one of the blessings of friendships among children for whom the language of reason has not yet displaced that of the heart. At any rate, it suited everyone, including the Sisters whom I wrongly suspected of wanting to supplant my mother in my affections.

Why? I could not really tell. Maybe because of a premature and somewhat tactless suggestion that I should take advantage of the sampling of mothers which the orphanage offered. The truth is that many of the feelings which determine our understanding of people and things defy any logic. In any case, the very idea of a comparison between the Sisters and my mother seemed to me the ultimate sacrilege.

Dead, my mother was still my mother. It was for her I longed, for her I wept, for her, the unique, the irreplaceable one who bore in her the perfect knowledge of my being and, in the words of an old Lebanese proverb, whose "heart had seen me long before her eyes."

I wanted my mother and I also wanted my father, my two brothers and my two sisters—my family, that radiant nest in whose bosom we all felt bundled up in warmth and so exquisitely alive.

With them gone, the whole world did not make the slightest sense anymore. And I made even less.

To the Sisters' patient overtures, I responded by lowering my eyes, and I shut my eyes altogether when they attempted too direct an approach. I was aware of their grieved sighs and I couldn't have cared less. They came from too far away. Counting on time, the well-known healer of many wounds, they resigned themselves to questioning Jad: "Has he had enough to eat? Does he like apples? He is so pale all of a sudden. Do you think he is not feeling well? Has he understood the grammar lesson?"

Jad answered yes...no...not at all...he did not understand the past tense...he has finished his arithmetic, and so on.

I felt these dialogues were about a child who wasn't there, and when Jad backed up his statements with "Isn't it, Naseem?" I didn't even think of nodding. He could say anything he pleased: only his presence mattered. Near this cheerful, lively and talkative boy, I felt a little less anguished and lost. Hardly two weeks had gone by since my arrival at the orphanage and I was tagging at his heels everywhere he went. He never complained about it.

*   *   *

One Saturday afternoon, while we were waiting for our turn in the bath, he showed me a picture of his mother.

"My Mama was the prettiest mama in the world," he said. "I can't believe she is dead and I will never see her again. You know, I didn't see her dead, nor my little sister, Jihan, who has gone with her. I was at school when it happened. And my Papa, he was wounded. There were too many deaths at home that day. That's why my Papa had to send me here. You know, I wanted to die, too."

He put away the picture in a prayerbook which he kept under his pillow and began to weep silently. Of course, I wept with him, for the same devastating pain made us want to die there, both of us, sitting on the floor between our beds. After a while, Jad put his book on my lap and said, "It was my Mama's prayerbook. My Papa gave it to me so that I would have something from her. You know, your Mama must also have been the prettiest in the world, and it's awful not to have any souvenir from her. If you want, we'll share my book. A bit mine, a bit yours. You'll see, there are lots of pictures in it. Oh! I hate the war! Tomorrow, when I am grown-up, I will do any kind of work against war. Do you think there is such a thing? Anyway, we'll do it together. My Papa will agree, I am sure."

Jad kept on talking for a long time, but I wasn't listening anymore. I stroked the book with a grateful hand. I could have mistaken it for my own mother's—it looked so much like it. And I felt as though Jad was offering me something she had actually touched.

4

At school, Jad was doing extremely well, although he certainly did not seem to be exerting himself. But I had a very hard time keeping up, to say the least. I would nod over my books and let my mind wander. I was supposed to write scraps of lessons of which I did not remember a single word. The rest of the time, I could let my dreams run wild without any fear of a surprise oral test.

"Come on, write," Jad urged me. "What shape is the earth? Come on, you know it. It's round like a ball."

Of course, I knew it. My Jeddo had told me, up there on the hill. Well, it was very hard for me to admit, as a fact, that everything in the whole world could hold onto a floating ball without ever falling off into space. The "force of gravity" (I remembered this term all the better for its fantastic sound) remained a mystery to me. But I wouldn't dream of questioning my Jeddo's word. To me, anything he said was at once invested with the force of truth.

Rather than write, I chewed on my pen, abandoning myself to my private questions: "The earth is round like a ball. And my village, with its hill, round like half of a ball, is a tiny bit of the earth. An obliterated bit of the earth. How could it be that no one remained up there? Did the sun still rise above our mountains? Did it bathe the charred stones of our houses in its light? What could its rays be like when they swept over a dead village?" I pictured a black sun shrouding the petrified silence of our home, and fear again gripped my stomach like a vise. In the cold silence where I let myself sink, my breathing became oppressed and my blood pounded in my temples. Jad's indignant whisper exploded in my ears:

"What? You haven't begun to write? What are you thinking of? An F, is that what you want?"

I looked hesitantly toward him, like a drowning man trying to reach out to the drifting boat passing by.

"Oh, St. Elijah," he sighed, "I'll bet you were back there again! Here." (His pen was racing on a sheet of paper.) "Copy that and get on with it, will you!"

Ah, yes, in the face of my inertia, Jad, normally so good, found no other way to cope than cheating. He was cheating out of love, whether all the schoolmasters in the world might like it or not, and, strangely, neither he nor I were conscious of doing anything wrong. I took great pains (that was the least I could do), to copy his scribbling as carefully as I could.

One evening, however, he explained:

"Listen, Naseem." (That was always his opening line for serious statements.) "Listen, Naseem, you don't do a blasted thing, and maybe you can't help it. I cheat, and something here (he hit his chest with his fist) tells me that Mama wouldn't scold me if I could tell her. Anyway, when my Papa comes, I'll tell him. He won't scold me either, I am sure, except maybe he won't like it very much.

"Listen, Naseem, one day you will speak again and, like it or not, you'll have to recite your lessons. Yesterday, at the medical checkup, I came just after you, remember? And when I walked in, the doctor was telling the Sister that nothing was damaged in you; that your voice might come back any time; that one had to be patient. Then the Sister said: 'Look, here is Jad, his friend.' Then the doctor asked me if you never said even a single word when we were alone and if you cried a lot and all that. I said, 'No, he speaks neither for real nor in his sleep.'

"But since yesterday, lots of things have been churning in my head. I am thinking, Oh, St. Elijah, how hard I am thinking! I can't tell you all of it but I'll tell you one thing: I cheat because if you flunk, you will have to repeat the year.

And if you do, just think, if I'm still here next year, we wouldn't be in the same grade anymore. Can you imagine that? Can't you make a little effort?"

No, I couldn't bear to imagine that and I was crushed. At that very minute, I understood what Jad had come to represent for me. I couldn't do without him anymore. Without knowing it, I loved him very much. Oh, St. George, there I was, loving again. I loved someone who was alive and whom I could see, hear, and touch. I clung to him like ivy to a wall. He had become my family. And now, he was talking of parting, of leaving.

My heart began to pound from love and despair. What did I care if I had to repeat a grade two, three, or four times since his father would come some day to fetch him anyway. Sooner or later, he would come. Jad did not doubt it, and neither did I. Was I going to drown again in loneliness just when I had caught sight of a star?

I could not suppress the sobs that shook my whole body. If Jad left, I might as well remain mute and, on top of that, become blind and deaf, or even lose my sense of touch for the rest of my life.

Jad slipped out of his covers and shook my arm: "Don't cry, you idiot. I'll never leave you. I swear it on my mother's grave. Don't you see, I am cheating to stay with you? And when my father takes me away, I won't leave you either." I tried as hard as I could, but I couldn't see how Jad would manage to follow his father and yet not leave me.

Meanwhile, I still wasn't studying a thing. As soon as I sat down at my desk, my thoughts flew back to my village. I fought as hard as I could to thrust aside my vision of the black sun. Instead, in my mind, I strolled slowly through the streets, delighting in the sight of the houses, which I had seen crumbled, rising again as if by magic. A wonderful blue cupola opened out on a happy world. The gardens were in bloom again, and the people were gesturing as they had before death. I could hear their voices and all the noises which tell of the liveliness of a village without war.

Allah! How those old days glittered in my ecstatic dreams! I traveled back through time on the song of a flute. Suddenly I was five again, begging my father to let me go with him to the town where he often went on business.

He left with the first morning bus and only came back at sunset, with his pockets full of small surprises which we would fish out ourselves.

"One pocket for each," he would say, lifting his arms. "You must find which one."

That was easy enough, for the places where he put his purchases were always the same. "My" pocket was inside his coat, where he kept his wallet. I would eagerly reach into it, thrilled with anticipation and never disappointed when I pulled out the small trifle which was mine.

Sometimes, during the holidays, he would take with him one of my older brothers or sisters. Their joy was such that I begged for my turn insistently, refusing to admit that I was still too young. One evening, he gave way to my persistence.

The next morning, we woke up at the crack of dawn. I was seething with excitement at what promised to be a most extraordinary journey. My father was his usual calm self, but my mother was nervous and worried as if I were about to depart for China. She kissed me, called me her soul, her house, her eyes, her heart, her life. She smoothed my hair with her fingers which felt lighter than a cloud. She traced the sign of the cross on my forehead, straightened my shirt collar and flooded my father with warnings:

"Take care of the boy. Don't let him stick his head or arms out of the bus window. Don't let go of his hand under any circumstances in the streets—you might lose him. If he perspires, don't give him ice-cold orangeade, and if your friends take it into their heads to make him drink the slightest drop of arak* or coffee, they'll hear from me. Here is his basket. I fixed him some bread and jam, fruit and cookies. Oh, St. George, I won't live until you get back!"

My father answered calmly enough at first, "As you wish, my wife! Whatever you say will be." But in the end, he grew impatient and cried out, "Enough! Your son is also mine. Do you think you're leaving him in strange hands? As you leave him, so you will find him. After all, you're hurting my feelings by insinuating that I don't know how to take care of him. The first time I take a child away from you for a minute, you act like I'm taking away your soul! How were the others when I brought them back to you? Weren't they just the same as when I'd taken them away? Strengthen your heart, please, and give us your blessing."

"Strengthen my heart!" my mother replied in an offended tone, calling on the neighbors as witness. "Oh neighbors, look at him! Listen to him! May Allah help us when men cannot understand women's feelings!"

"May Allah help *us* with women," my father replied with a laugh.

I laughed too. I was rather surprised for, after all, in the village, children were free as kings. We went where we pleased, without any adult supervision. We would caper about to our heart's content and then walk (perspiring) into any house where we'd drink large glasses of ice water mixed with blackberry, cherry or rose syrup. And on feast days, we were allowed a bit of arak—just enough to get a notion of what it tasted like. Why was all this to be prohibited in town? And what was there to fear when I was with my father anyway?

Allah! How sweet those memories were. And how painful. How we loved our mother's tender concern and our father's tranquil strength.

---

*A Lebanese liquor made of fermented raisins and anise.

"The truth is," my father said, once we had settled ourselves in the bus, "I would have been very worried if your mother hadn't made her usual scene. It's a good thing indeed that a woman wears her heart on her sleeve. It's good for all of us."

Yes, my father, it was good, it was delicious, it was the honey of our lives. It was...and now it no longer is!

Jad's voice forced me back into this world which my whole being rejected:

"Oh, St. Elijah, what have I done to you that you've stuck this slug of a Naseem on me to put up with? All I ask him to do is copy, and look how he dawdles. I can't write in his place, can I?"

5

About St. Elijah, St. Abda, St. Sasseen, or any other saints particularly venerated in Lebanon, I believe some explanation is in order.

Jad firmly believed that St. Elijah, his village's patron saint, was the greatest saint of all time—past, present, and future. I believed just as firmly that St. George, my village's patron, could never be rivalled, on earth or in heaven.

But I obligingly tolerated Jad's delusion and, when he heard which saint I depended upon, he showed the same gracious condescension. After all, to each village, its own patron saint and thus its belief in the supremacy of its chosen one among the chosen. Besides, everyone knows that when your own patron saint doesn't heed your prayers, calling to the one from the next village or from even further away can't be of any help. He has his reasons which, in the depth of your heart, you can very well guess, even if you pretend not to understand it at all. And don't fool yourself, there isn't a thing any other saint can do about it.

The fact is the patron saint of a village is not just "two grains." He is worth his weight in incense "and a half" which, in Lebanese, means "and more!"

He sits up there at the right hand of the Father...well, just after the Holy Virgin, that is!

He is holier than all the saints of heaven, and his miracles are more numerous and better than those of all the saints put together, except for the Virgin's, who is the only one capable of outdoing him on every level.

His powers stop just short of advising God himself, for, along with his virtues, his powers are everything I mentioned above "and a half!" At any rate, you could never find a more diligent or efficient mediator.

Without him, the village would be lacking something essential, impossible to define yet as indispensable as daily bread.

People whose faith and reason will stoop only too rarely to a little detour through sentiment might find all this rather strange. It's too bad, for they are depriving themselves of a refinement of perception, of relationships and of spiritual well-being which no analysis—never mind how rigorous and well-constructed—can ever bring them.

As for us, the Lebanese from the mountain, we are so much under the spell of irrationality that we hold that the heart is the first among the senses and only consider the five other ones (plus reason) as wonderful tools in the service of the first.

But let's come back to our local saints. If any memories can immerse me back into village euphoria, those of the feast of our St. George are the ones.

On the eve of that glorious day, tradition demanded thunder, wind and rain, at least for a few minutes. This was not seen as a natural phenomenon to be expected at that time of the year, but as an obvious sign of our saint's powers.

As soon as morning came, we would scrutinize the horizon in search of a storm-laden cloud. And when it descended upon us, we strutted around, showing off, happy to be able to deprive the followers of St. Abda and St. Sasseen and others of the pleasure of insinuating that our St. George had become a powerless old saint.

If, by chance (and this was a rare occurrence, for nothing is more faithful than a tradition), there was no thunder around our steeple, we were ready to swear that our saint was busy riding above another parish of the same allegiance whose faith in his power might have been wavering a bit. Our faith didn't need any proofs, did it? Nevertheless, our pride would feel a slight pinch of disappointment, but this was soon replaced by a deep surge of joy and prayer.

Preparations for feasts always began way ahead of time. They opened with a novena of evening Masses which gave the whole village an opportunity to come together. After Mass, our priest stood in front of the main altar, facing the congregation, and displayed a large framed picture of our saint, the way he would hold up the monstrance during processions. In front of him, an altar boy would swing the incense burner in an ample and majestic gesture which followed the rhythm of hymns to the glory of St. George sung by the whole assembly.

The children sat on the steps of the sanctuary and sometimes rocked to the rhythm of the old melodies which the smell of incense and the flickering candlelight made deeper and more undulating. Some of them would fall asleep with their heads on their folded arms, and their parents would step forward to cover them up with shawls or coats so they wouldn't catch cold.

We also made preparations at home. The women would wash the holiday tablecloths and polish anything that happened to be in their paths. They washed the floors, the doors, the windows; they kneaded cakes and breads; they hustled the men who tried hopelessly to get out of their way. They put flowers on the tables, bureaus and shelves, until the dawn of the great day finally arrived.

From noon till midnight at least the two church bells rang in full peal. All the male villagers from the five or six year-olds to the oldest bent Jeddo took endless turns at the rope.

How heavy they were, those bells. How hard to set in motion. The children got together in swarms like bees getting ready to leave their hive. And when they all tumbled down together, that indeed made a remarkable mess of arms, legs, laughs, shouts and protests.

Tradespeople from the vicinity, and sometimes from farther away, would appear and take over the church square with their displays of cakes, fireworks, and an astonishing variety of tiny toys which seemed particularly appealing on that day.

Allah, how lively it was! What an explosion of joy when dusk twinkled with all our lights. The church was full to bursting. We walked endlessly in and out, a firework stick in one hand, a cotton swab dipped in holy water in the other. There was plenty of running, singing, praying, chasing, catching, swirling, popping of firecrackers, greetings, and meditating all over the place. At last, the Mass began and it ended in a dizzying stirring of emotion which was a far cry from the devotion of Christmas or the solemnity of Easter. But this noisy, surging fervor was no less intense.

Our sectarianism, however, did not prevent us from celebrating some other saint, some other day in some other parish, or from bringing back a few grains of incense and drops of holy water from those feasts. We would show the same respect when we ran our hands over the images venerated by our neighbors and crossed our foreheads, lips and breasts for their patron saints. We did it because we liked to pray, to get together, to laugh, to dance, and to cry with those who cry. We liked to offer and receive sweets, to offer the light of our homes and taste that of others.

We enjoyed simple pleasures. Pleasures which came at the slightest inducement because they came from deep inside us. One hears of austere people, of rational people, of great and superior people, of miserly people or pretentious people. We were a people of happiness, naive and carefree and clever, ready to trust the slightest smile, to take miracles and wonders for granted just as we did the sun and the rain.

And now, our villages are gone. No path can lead us back to them but the path of memories.

Oh, St. George, how heartbreaking are the memories in exile!

6

No, I wasn't at all getting used to the kind of reality which was forced upon me. How does one get used to a tornado which throws a whole country into horror?

For the time being, the orphanage was sheltered in the hollow of a valley, but the ongoing violence kept us all aghast. We couldn't escape the echoes of the blasts that shook the nights. The horrors of the war reached us through the transistor radios to which the teachers kept listening, even in the courtyard at recess time; through the newspapers which the Sisters were silently reading; through some of the children who would spend the weekend at home and come back with tales horrible enough to paralyze your soul for the rest of your life; through the news flashes (when there was electricity) in the lounge where we were allowed to watch television on Saturday nights—it never left us.

In the midst of some story which we would all be watching with passionate interest, to try to forget for the moment that our reality was quite different, wham! horror suddenly burst through the screen, through our eyes and ears, through our fragile sense of safety.

In red and black—red, like my family's blood! Black like the smoke billowing over the agony of our village!

Ah! I was scared, and I was not alone. We all had first-hand knowledge of the exodus, the kidnappings, the tortures. We all knew of the corpses torn apart under the crumbled houses or on the roads. The children had no tears left to cry.

What I feared was not death—I no longer felt really alive anyway—but the hatred which forced itself upon me with the reality of the war.

*   *   *

Oh my father, my mother, what finally was the truth?
Was it the too beautiful dream we had once called "home"
or was it the war whose savage assaults over the whole
world I was beginning to experience?

Were you only a dream, you who would tell me that love
is the light of the earth and teach me to join my hands as if
to join heaven and earth together?

No, such warmth, such tenderness, such happiness and
sunshine could not possibly have been only in our imagination, for it had been given to us and we had known it. This
happiness of yesterday—I had known it with my eyes, my
ears, my sense of smell, of touch, of taste, and a thousand
undefinable sensations which gave my heart its true life. I
had known the sweet security one could feel while cavort-
ing freely within the tenderness of one's family.

I had known the affectionate teasing of Yussef, my elder
brother whom I admired almost as much as I did my father,
and Lamia's spirited impulses, Milad's insatiable curiosity
which prompted him to take my mother's iron apart to see
how it worked, and the sweet grace of Hala whom my
father called his velvet kitten.

I had known the subtle differences of each dawn as the
seasons changed, and the peace of sunsets which opened
onto the stars. I had known the sea and the long silvery
furrow which the moon traced on it as it rose above the
mountains, round and veined with the color of honey.

I had known the soft pattering of the rain quenching the
earth's thirst, the rustle of each leaf in the wind, and the
sky in the autumn puddles over which we would bend as if
trying to catch hold of the clouds.

I had known the noises of morning and evening, and the
voices and steps of all our village's inhabitants.

Was all that lost forever?

One day, it occurred to me that the whole village could
not possibly have perished all at once. Some survivors

must be left. Who? Where had they found refuge? How could they be reached?

"My father, my mother," I prayed, as a mad hope came over me, "let me see at least one person whose voice would pronounce your names, who would tell of yesterday's evenings with the neighbors and the stories about the lives of each one of them. I used to pay so little attention to them, and now I am trying to piece them together into a mosaic which would bring back the story of my lost paradise in clear vignettes."

For I knew nothing of you, my father, my mother. I knew nothing of your childhood, of your joys and your sufferings, of your dreams, of your deep secret being which had shaped us, your children.

What does one really grasp of the persons one loves the most on earth? Which word, which gesture, which glance might unveil for us the essence of a soul had we not overlooked it? Why are we sometimes overcome by the aching nostalgia of what has escaped us and is buried inside such a deeply bitter "never again"?

I know now that your son does not need to peer into your faces to reach what cannot be put into words. I know now that what passed from you to me, what you poured into me by loving me the way you did, fed my roots a kind of nourishment which could only bring about one choice for life—even through your deaths.

And to this day, although you are now long gone and the war is still with us, I cannot bear to think of letting myself slip into hatred and violence. For what is by essence destruction cannot save anything at all, least of all life itself.

My father, my mother, I have touched hell and am still touching it in this endless war one thousand times more fierce and fatal than it was in its beginnings. And I see children much more deeply wounded than I was.

In their presence, sometimes, I feel overcome by despair and powerlessness to the point of thinking that screaming, biting and hitting blindly would work better than anything else. But your voices in me remind me that any form of violence is an acceptance of war, and that to children stabbed by hatred, only floods of tenderness can give back their smile.

Thus, for you and through you, through the love which you infused into me from my coming into this world, and with which you guided my first steps, I refuse to ever become myself a tool of destruction.

For you, through you, I believe that love is the light of the world and that prayer can join heaven to earth.

I believe it because you could not possibly have misled the one you called the light of your souls. I believe it because my childhood near you was much too tenderly happy for me to ever doubt it.

*   *   *

At seven, however, I could not bear to have become nobody's son and to be lost in a confused mass of coralled children who hardly knew anymore whether they had a right to expect anything else.

Little by little, I came to notice that many of them cried at night, softly, noiselessly, their tears flowing, slow and heavy, like bells endlessly tolling their distress. Whispers also reached my ears, and the furtive patter of small bare feet, and laughs smothered into pillows. Each had his own way of reaching out a hand to others and bracing themselves for the long desert of the night.

Finally, sleep stretched out its silence. Sister Marie made a last round, picked up a wandering pillow, covered a shivering shoulder, stroked a face still wet with tears. I could hear her coming and hid my face under my covers. How many times she stopped by my bed! Her hand would lightly run through my hair, but I wouldn't move. Why should I? Nothing could relieve my boundless loneliness.

My father, my mother, I am only telling what your orphaned little boy was feeling: an unbearable severance from the permanence of love, the sort of permanence which can hardly be expected in an orphanage too full of children, themselves too full of problems, of fears, of nightmares.

How could we have understood that an orphanage is not a home? With more than two hundred urchins, some of them mulish or peevish, others sluggish or weepy, discipline was a must under penalty of chaos. And feelings, like everything else, must be bound by the schedule. But it should not be surprising that a scheduled caress does not automatically arouse a scheduled response.

Sister Marie may well touch my hair; there was no way she could touch my heart. Not for lack of trying—but what could we have done about it, either of us?

When the night terrified me, after her rounds were through, it was time for Sister Marie and her sweet smile to be with her community. This world of hers was parallel to ours and could in no way ever blend with ours, ruled as it was by its own laws and prayers: the mute symmetry of its own order, its uniformity of expressions and clothes, its controlled impulses and its impervious slices of time which seemed to us so secret—times for services, for meals, for sleep ("Do you think they sleep like our Mamas?" asked Jad), times for recreation, times for meetings, and a perpetual frenzy to be on schedule. "Hurry! hurry! We must be done before the bell rings...before the end of the week...before the end of the term."

We felt so far from our homes, and everything seemed to be done with. But what was there to be done with, I ask you? Crying...loving...living? What were you done with, my father, my mother, at the time of your deaths? What was our village done with? Nothing, least of all living.

To be done for the sake of being done! Papa, you used to

say, when we botched our homework or our prayers, that if such was the case, we might as well not have begun—it now seems to me it only means shattering oneself into a million little ends...a million little deaths.

And to live! Mama, you used to say that all there was to it was love. It now seems to me that to love as you did means to dissolve oneself into the never-ending abundance of all that is celebrating life: from the fragrance of orange trees to the kisses you used to nestle into your baskets; to the seed which is only buried so that it will come back to life in a sheaf; even to death, that other sleep that comes before the Easter of all those who, like you and my father, know how to keep Love from the limits of time and measure.

My father, my mother, I missed you too much, and Sister Marie could do nothing. All of us cried every night, for we were snatched too soon from a feeling most necessary and reassuring for a child—the feeling of belonging to beings who he believes also belong to him forever.

We were snatched from a home where a child would never find himself crying alone, where he would fall asleep cuddled in his mother's arms, with her warmth close to his small heart. And if he was frightened in his sleep, or thirsty, or not feeling well, he could call out the wonderful name which encompasses all the sweetness in the world—Mama!

At every hour of the day or night...Mama!

Sometimes, for no other reason than the joy of knowing her close enough to hear his cry...Mama!

To sleep, cradled in one's mother's arms when one is sick, and to hear one's father's voice nearby on the big bed: "Oh, my wife, is the boy still burning up? Are you sure it's nothing serious? If something happens to him, I will lose my mind!"

Papa's weakness and his sudden incompetence in the face of our childhood illnesses, and Mama's appeasing strength. This double tenderness bending over my fever.

This double assurance of love with two names. This all-transparent communication where no one knows clearly where the one begins or the other ends. This intimacy melted into a unique certainty.

And my brothers and sisters exclaiming in the morning: "Have the little chick's feathers been smoothed? Will he be able to parade in the sun?"

A family!

My family!

*　　*　　*

"Which of your children do you love the most?" goes a Lebanese saying.

"The little one until he grows up, the departed one until he comes back, the sick one until he recovers."

7

Once, my father did almost lose his mind. That was when my mother had pleurisy.

Papa despised the principle according to which a man must not show his feelings too much. He expressed his joys, his worries and his affection in words and gestures. With him, we always knew where we stood and it was very reassuring. And if Mama did wear her heart on her sleeve, Papa's heart was poured out on all the members of his family, most of all on his tender but firm better half.

Another saying of ours specifies that "A man is the head of his wife," meaning, no doubt, that it is the woman who holds up her husband's head on her own shoulders so that she can turn it any way she pleases! And without Mama's shoulders, Papa would have seen the world upside down. Such was, at any rate, what he said when, after ten days of panic, our family finally returned to its normal pace.

Nothing was going right any longer under the roof of our father. Just think—our mother was sick! "A nasty case of pleurisy," diagnosed the doctor when he was summoned on that memorable morning. Papa had (unwittingly, upon his honor!) snored until after seven o'clock while the house was creeping with an unusual silence. Don't think that my father was always the last one to get up, but, on that day, his nostrils had not been tickled as usual by the aroma of freshly brewed coffee; his ears had not been pleasantly aroused by the familiar noises of breakfast being prepared in the kitchen; and no child's laugh had made his heart leap with joy. As a result, Papa only emerged from his dreams when he had slept his fill "and a half." He stretched himself, praised the Lord, glanced at his watch and held back with difficulty the outburst of rather ugly words which were rising on his lips.

"Allah," he crossed himself, "where did my wife go? Could it be that old Teta Zarifa has died? May misfortune stay away from us! What if Mama had to go out in the middle of the night? No, she would have let me know. And if she had, anyway, I would have heard her go out. I am not deaf yet, as far as I know. Allah! I don't like this silence," he said as he crossed himself again. "I am worried, very worried...very, very worried."

Papa rushed into our room. We were all still happily asleep, as one would have expected, perhaps unconsciously enjoying playing truant without it being our fault.

"Your glory, oh Allah," Papa sighed. "On holidays, they wake up before the birds. On school days they have to be shaken like pines in the Fall. But instead of pine nuts, we only collect yawns and grunts. Anyway, the heck with school."

In other words, this morning, our father did not care a pine nut about education. His wife was what he wanted, his wife in flesh and blood, with her exquisite morning smile and a pot of steaming coffee in her hand. No, by Allah, she should not disappear like that at the crack of dawn and leave her husband and children—the pillar of her house and the lights of her soul—in the most alarming ignorance as to her whereabouts.

He found her in the kitchen, crumpled up on a low stool, more pale and weak than anyone had ever seen her before.

"Kheir Insh'Allah!*" he blurted out, crossing himself for the third time as he knocked on the wood of the door in an attempt to chase away bad luck. "What's wrong with you, my wife?"

"I don't feel well," sighed Mama. "To tell you the truth, I can't stay on my feet."

"Your glory, oh Allah!" moaned Papa who (was it empathy or fear?) felt his own legs getting weak to the

*"Good news, God willing."

point that he, too, had to sit down. "Why didn't you wake me up? I'm going to get the doctor."

"No," Mama protested. "Don't even think of it. This is only a spell. Help me to get back to our room. A little rest and a good cup of coffee, and I'll be fine again."

"Are you sure?" asked Papa, who was more than willing to believe her and already began to take heart. "Don't think of anything. I'll take care of everything."

And Papa meant it, too. But when he got back into the kitchen...

"Where's the coffee?" he shouted. "Where's the sugar? How many spoonfuls of sugar do I put in? And how much coffee? Where are the cups? Where do you store the tray? By my children, it's too tidy around here, that's why I can't find anything!"

Finally, the coffee was ready, but Mama lay panting, weak and burning with fever.

"My wife is dying," Papa choked. He rushed to the window and called the nearest neighbor, begging her to call the doctor. He also needed his mother-in-law at once. She was wonderful at reassuring everybody and knew by heart all the potions, poultices, ointments and incantations that could heal all kinds of fevers. He also had to wake up the children and began uttering oaths. No, by St. George, never had he seen his wife in such a state. He lost his mind altogether and, according to Lamia, he began to wander around "like a gypsy who has lost her blue bead."*

Five minutes had not gone by when the house was swarming with people. The doctor shook his head as he tried to explain to our father, who seemed to hold the doctor responsible for this misfortune, that it was not *his* fault if Mama always did things to perfection, including having this pleurisy, with its rare and unusual side-effects,

---

*In Lebanon, many women wear a blue bead which is supposed to ward off the evil eye.

and that, for this reason, he could not predict its outcome. All he could do was "apply the eyedrops and Allah would take care of the blindness." And why hadn't Mama spoken sooner? After all, "if its going to rain, the sky gets cloudy," and pleurisy doesn't just come upon you in one second.

Papa, yellow as saffron, answered that one need not have spent so many years on the worm-eaten benches of an old university only to be unable to cure a simple cold. "A woman as strong as mine, never the flu, just good old colds; five children so full of their mother's milk all they need now is the morning dew, and you mean to tell me you don't understand a thing about the case? You *must* cure her for us, Doctor!"

I remember Papa's indignation. We stood around him, the five of us, completely stunned, but sharing totally in his "folly," because he was our father and our mother's life was at stake.

"Five chicks," Papa went on, "so small they could all take shelter under the same sieve, and you want them to become orphans? Doctor, their father begs you: do your duty. Heal their mother and our gratitude will follow you all the way to Saint Peter's gate!"

The next few days were lost to me in the kind of dream-like state which came over the house. My two Tetas settled themselves at Mama's bedside while neighbors tiptoed in and out bringing dishes and sweet desserts "to cheer up our hearts." My father would not touch them. "It's going to be all right, children, I promise you it'll be all right," he assured us in a voice we had never heard him use before.

Oddly enough, he took to tidying up his things, and even helped Lamia wash the dishes. In the evenings, we gathered together as usual for prayer time. Without Mama, Hala and I forgot the words a bit and the Blessed Virgin seemed quite remote. But we had no fears because we never doubted that Mama would recover.

What made us so sure? Our Tetas' smiles, Papa's words,

or a certainty in our own hearts? We thought time was dragging, but we knew that someday we would hear her voice again calling us "her life."

Then, one morning, Papa woke us up at dawn. He was crying, but his eyes shone like stars. "Ah! my little ones, " he said, "she's out of danger. She wants to see the five of you. Run and tell her how much you love her."

8

These memories! I wore them thin in my attempt to recreate the atmosphere of our home which I so sorely missed at the orphanage. As days went by, life (if there was any left in this war) seemed more and more to go on somewhere else, far from these walls inside of which one never heard talk of births, weddings, christenings, sheep, or the harvests.

Who was the baker who kneaded the bread we ate? Where did the spring sing that gave us our water? Where did the clothes we wore come from? Who washed them, ironed them, darned them? Who would lay a kiss on a torn shirt?

Anonymous hands folded anonymous clothes, numbered like our cubbyholes in the dorm or the rows of hooks where we hung our towels. This made it all so impersonal.

I imagined a seamstress crying with impatience: "That number 206 is really too much! He always has the largest holes in his socks." But maybe I'm exaggerating and perhaps she would sigh with a touch of compassion: "This poor orphan, if only he could be a little more careful!"

Holes, there were some in my memories, too. Some nights, I could not find my family's living faces anymore. Their death masks forced themselves upon me and would not leave me. I tried as hard as I could to think of something else. I conjured up the amber landscapes of our holidays, the acrid smell of the still pines through the sunny summers, the chirping of the katydids, gorged with sun and sap, the song of the spring, warbling like a laugh of secret happiness, our games of hide-and-seek in the church square: "...ninety-eight, ninety-nine, one hundred and the red rose opens!"

We would hide as far as the neighboring houses, entering through the back doors and going out through the front. On the way, we would be offered fruit, a piece of cake, or pistachio nuts. Of course, when the "seeker" inquired from door to door, from garden to garden, no one had ever seen anyone. He then came back savoring a peach, not the least bit disappointed to find us all back at "base." Sometimes one would manage to catch everybody and the stampede through the gardens resembled an olympic race.

Where were they, those children from home, squirrels of the woods which they filled with their sunny laughter, with signs, and with stories of their discoveries: of bird's nests in which they couldn't stop watching the lovely mottled eggs, beetles with pearly glints of light, tiny light yellow grasshoppers which they would disturb on purpose in order to glimpse a flash of the colors of their inside wings—blue, red, orange, yellow, green—so beautiful one would feel like catching them to make rainbows.

With all my strength, I called back these memories of light, but death remained looming over my bed. It erased the songs, the colors, and the faces to make me the prisoner of fear again.

*   *   *

What were the children's games in the orphanage's yard? I didn't care. Sitting on my bench, I stared at the sky. Ah! to be able to lie on a cloud and drift in the pure blue sky. To be a bird and fly over seas and mountains. To go away from the war. To think only of chasing the wind. To have wings—how wonderful! By the way, do birds know how to dodge shells?

I was pondering this question when a loud "Bang," screamed by a frenzied Ramzi, struck my ears like the explosion of a real gun. He had made my bench into a barricade, and used my shoulder as the swivel base for his "machine gun"—an invisible weapon with which he sprayed three little tykes who were facing me with their hands up, looking more thrilled than frightened.

War as a game...a raised fist with the thumb up and the index finger pointed at the enemy, who can't wait to fall to the ground in grand style...a triumphant cry: "Bang, bang, you're dead!"

Death as a game...to swirl and fall flat on one's face with one's eyes closed, but still chewing on a piece of strawberry flavored gum while agonizing cheerfully: "Ouch! Ouch! I'm dead!"

Make believe war.

Make believe death.

And suddenly, death for real. Death—to cry and die.

But the war dead did not close their eyes. I had seen them, I could still see them—gaping eyes suddenly emptied of their tenderness. There, in front of me, lay the members of my family, sprawled between those four urchins who, because they had never seen the war, could play at it with delight.

Bang! Bang! Bombs were raining on my house and my whole family fell together. I alone was left alive. It seemed absurd and not true...no, not true! Allah! If only it were not true!

The sky suddenly spun and all disappeared....

I woke up in the infirmary with Sister Marie's hand on my forehead and Jad's sniffles at the foot of my bed. I opened my eyes and he began to yelp like a wounded puppy: "Cross my heart, I thought you were dead. No, please, don't go again. Please, wake up for good! Oh, St. Elijah, you scared me so!"

"Come now, Jad, pull yourself together," said Sister Marie. "There, there, it's all over. He is fine. Tell me, how was he feeling this morning? Did you notice anything in particular?"

"No, he was just like he is every morning—half awake, half asleep."

He sat by my side and watched me thoughtfully. I wanted to tell him, "Jad, don't leave me. Not you. Never. I will do anything you want, but please, please, don't ever leave me."

The words did not come out. So, I hid my face in my pillow and, for the first time, I cried in front of one of the Sisters.

Jad took my hand and said, "He's not ill. He's been frightened."

"Of what?" asked Sister Marie sharply. "What frightened him? What happened in the yard?"

"Nothing," said Jad. "He is afraid of the war."

Sister Marie tried to take me in her arms, but I resisted so violently that she had to give up.

"Stay with him, Jad," she said. "I think he really needs you."

My hand in Jad's, I sank into a dreamless sleep.

*　　　*　　　*

I remember a drawing Jad did one evening at study while I was busy copying some grammar exercises. He tore a double sheet ("to have more space") from the center of his copybook. On it, he drew red-roofed houses with green shutters, flowers, and an orchard whose trees bore more cherries and apples than they had leaves. Under the trees, a man was sowing, and a fistful of seeds was raining from his hand. The sky was of a splendid dark blue shade which made one long to get lost inside it. On the right, a yellow sun darted its slanted rays on a woman carrying a child. On the left, a crescent moon was floating among the stars. There was even a small cloud from which rain fell softly in the dazzling sky.

His drawing seemed so beautiful, so cheerful, that I felt I was drinking straight from a spring.

"This is our home," Jad said, his lips quivering with nostalgia. "Here is my father, and there is my mother with my little sister, Jihan. When I think of home, I always remember good weather. When I was born, my father slaughtered a sheep and he treated the whole village to it. And my Jeddo rang the bells for my christening himself. One day, we'll go back there. My Papa has told me so. I don't know if I'll want to go back into the house without my Mama. I don't think I can. There, this is a present. I drew it for you."

I stared at his "home," fascinated by the light which poured from it. It was too beautiful, too intense, too much like my home. It was another world, our world, where war was utterly meaningless.

My father, my mother, my brothers, my sisters, my village: all of a sudden you were present, with Jihan and her mother, around Jad and myself who could think of nothing but you. I felt your presence. I couldn't bear your silence.

Mama, my heart begged, one word, only one. Let me hear your voice calling me "your life." You too were my life. I could have told you that a hundred times a day. But children don't know how to express those things until it's too late.

And you, Papa, did you slaughter a sheep when I was born? Such a beautiful thing, a birth, all the more so when it has been awaited with respect, and a sense of wonder and love.

You had told us of your joy, five times renewed. You had told us how your whole being was overwhelmed with emotion at the good news of your first-born. Mama would laugh and tease you when you were recounting what you called our "coming to you," to the world, to life. And we wanted to know, and to listen a hundred times to the same story. Because something in your voice—an emotion we could not fully understand, a joy which enchanted us— took us right inside your joy to have us.

And Mama's smile as she looked at us all...her smile

from inside that same joy...her contemplative smile as in a new "Annunciation."

Years and years of war, Papa. So many years since you left me. An eternity. And the war is still with us. Tonight, shells are raining by the thousands. More people killed. More people wounded. More children atrociously torn. Why this madness, Papa? I have grown up, but I am still afraid. For all these years we have seen only ruin and death. If you could know how hard it is not to give oneself up to it when one's soul is devastated. We can't go on. But I don't want to hate, Papa. I don't want to kill. I don't want to enter that circle of death, for I am your son and you taught me that life only exists through love.

So I say, as I used to in the old days: "Tell me, Papa. Tell me of life and births. Tell me of simple happiness and of the sun, forever present like a king behind the clouds, and the trees at dawn, when their leaves bear the mark of the silent night until the bird song stirs them to the light of day. Tell me of the mulberry tree in our garden which, you said, knew whose hands were stroking it, and of Mama's bouquets in the Spring which made the house fragrant with the thoughts that had occurred to her as she was picking them for us.

Tell me in the third person, as you used to, to better describe your family and blend yourself into its whole. Because you felt that when you said "I," you gave the impression that you were on one side and we on the other, and because your stories were so simply, wonderfully true that you told them to us as one would tell a tale.

Tell me, Papa. Did you really want so badly to have a son for your first child, you who used to say that a home without daughters is a garden without roses?

Tell me, my Papa. Tell of the time when you couldn't believe your eyes, or your ears....

9

Najm could not believe his eyes, or his ears: he was holding in his big, hard hands his first-born son who squealed enough to break anybody's heart.

Nine months! For nine months he had been waiting for that cherub. For nine months he had pictured him, smooth and pink and silky, all smiles and babbles...the image of his mother. And here he found himself, rocking a perfect stranger whose face was wrinkled, contorted and red with anger as he screamed at the top of his lungs. He tried to rock him gently from left to right...up and down...but, far from abating, the shrieks reached alarming new heights. The cherub finally gasped, struggled for his breath and Najm, in a panic, put him down into his wife's arms.

"Oh, my wife," he said, himself choking, "the baby is gone! Do something!"

Saida rested her son against her shoulder and gently patted his back while she murmured a nameless tune. At once, the child breathed a deep sigh of relief and sank into a blessed sleep.

Najm watched them both, dumbfounded. Wasn't that just like a man, he thought to himself, to lose the North, the South, the East and the West *and* to lose face on top of it all because of a newborn baby's cries. By St. George, he felt his dignity was slipping away fast and he tried in vain to salvage it with loud cries of "Allah! Allah!" and smoothed his handsome, curly moustache. His wife's mocking laughter made him feel like nothing more than a mouse.

"May Allah help us with men," she sang. "Tall, strong, brave, intelligent..."

"And what else," interjected Najm. "I know your litany

by heart. You'd better put the child back into his bed.
You're holding him like a sack, and I don't want a son as
twisted as a slug."

"Well," she answered back cheerfully, "after all, we'd
know whom he takes after!"

"And who is that, pray tell?" Najm inquired foolishly,
sure as he could be that there was nothing at all in common
between himself, erect as a yew tree and as strong as an
oak, and the possible distortion of his progeny's back.

"From his father and his twisted mind," the sweet
mother cooed.

Pow! With Saida there was no way to have the last word.
His honey, his rose of Eden, had only one thorn—she
always had a ready answer tucked under her arm. Logical
or not, that was beside the point. And now that she had
ensured the perpetuation of her family, she could indulge
in it to her heart's content.

Najm's feelings were ruffled, but he made no reply. He
did not want to risk upsetting his wife for fear of making
her milk turn sour. And, deep inside, he was very proud of
his budding family. No, there wasn't another baby in the
world who could scream with such power, gag, and then
fall asleep only two seconds later as if nothing had
happened.

And Saida, when had she acquired the tranquil and perfect assurance she displayed in all her gestures and sounds
she made at the baby? After all, she was only seventeen,
and this was her first child, born the day before, almost
without any warning, while the sun was beginning to sink
into the horizon.

Najm was working in the fields, thinking of his wife and
praying to St. George for a delivery without complications.

"Oh, St. George," he begged, suddenly overcome by a
superstitious fear, "forget a little how I pestered you with

my prayers that Heaven give me a son. If the mother and child are in good health, I will be grateful to you forever. But, if it has to be a girl, please let her look like her mother, and I guarantee she will be the light of my eyes."

Well, no use worrying. May unhappiness be far from us! Hadn't Saida's mother, mother-in-law, aunts, sisters, cousins and neighbors done their best to spare her any great strains? Hadn't they been vying with one another to protect her from any looks, gestures, or sayings which might have brought the evil eye upon her?

And Najm himself, although he did not believe much in what he termed "women's tales," hadn't he satisfied all her desires so as to spare the child any unsightly birthmarks? Proof: when Saida had expressed a sudden craving for raisins at eleven o'clock at night (Allah be my witness!) and there wasn't a single one left in the house, "Najm's head had not yet disappeared when his wife could see his feet again!" Imagine how fast he must have run to his neighbors who had provided him with a full bowl of beautiful brown raisins, with one thousand wishes as a bonus!

Oh, Lord, what a sight! What if the child had been born with a mark the shape of a raisin on his forehead, his cheek or his chin, or even on the tip of his nose! His father would be the one people would blame for it! Much worse still, Saida, his sweet Saida, for whom you could cross seven rivers and seven mountains without finding one like her, Saida would find it nearly impossible to forgive him for any suspect mark on the face of her "tender basil." Somewhere else on his body, maybe, but who can tell where frustrated cravings might become embedded? Neither you, nor me, nor anyone. So?

And when she had sighed: "A molasses cake, please, my husband. Oh, I can't help it. I have such a craving for one!"—at five o'clock in the morning, where were we to find one? May Allah help us with women! Saida could have waited for her mother-in-law's arrival. The trouble with cravings is that they do not respect any rules of place or time and that, in this case, the mother-to-be believed too much in their consequences.

Najm had run to the neighbor again, praying heaven to wake her up if she wasn't already awake. Luckily, she was sitting on her doorstep, grinding her coffee.

"A good morning to you, neighbor," Najm greeted her, touching his chest and then his forehead with his right hand. "Insh'Allah, that you may all be in good health."

"A morning of light to you, Najm," she replied. "What brings you here before daybreak? Nothing's wrong, I hope."

"Nothing's wrong, don't worry. Pray, forgive me, but if you or someone you know happened to have kneaded a molasses cake yesterday or the day before, I would be grateful if you could bring a piece to my wife. I will return the favor at the first opportunity, and may Allah shower his blessings on you, your household, and your children, and grant you long life and prosperity. A thousand thanks, but, without rushing you, may I beg you to hurry?"

"Don't worry, Najm. We know what it's like, and 'favors go both ways, just like two hands washing each other'." Go tell your wife that the cakes are as good as already in her house."

Five minutes later (the grapevine being to this day the fastest means of communication), six plates of molasses cakes were in Najm's house. Satisfied, and a trifle embarrassed, Saida smiled, thanked the neighbors, and passed coffee around while everyone recounted all the stories of cravings they had known since generations past.

Little by little, the house filled with women bringing friendly concern, curiosity, advice, coffee and extra cups in a deliciously colorful hubbub. The morning was getting off to an early start, to everyone's delight except Najm's who could do without it. He slipped away through the kitchen, grabbing a piece of cake on his way out, and longing for his usual morning bowl of labneh* crowned with springs of mint and shiny olives.

The child was due in the first part of April. The weather would be sunny (in the mountain, there was no such thing as a mistaken weather forecast), and Najm would offer arak in the garden—the arak which was saved for great occasions and which had been distilled three times. But the cherub must have been in a hurry to smell the fragrance of Spring flowers and to be sung to sleep by the little green frogs.

Najm was just pledging one pound of frankincense and three candles as big as the newborn infant when he spotted his cousin Asmahan galloping through the fields.

"Kheir Insh'Allah!" he stammered while he crossed himself with one hand and knocked on wood with the other (better two precautions than one!), for Asmahan's usual pace was sluggish as a turtle's and she generally seemed not to have any idea of what hurrying meant.

As soon as she saw Najm, Asmahan stopped. Breathless and flapping her fat arms in the air, she struggled to catch her breath and shouted: "Oh, Abu Yussef, Abu Yussef,** to you the good news, to me the helwayney***!"

Thus did Najm hear that his boy was born.

---

*a yoghurt spread
**After the birth of their first son, parents in Lebanon customarily are nicknamed "Father of . . ." (Abu) or "Mother of . . ." (Emm).
***Symbolic reward to the bearer of good news.

10

One Saturday afternoon at bath time, Jad was called into the parlor. He had been vigorously drying his hair with his towel. I saw him stop abruptly with his mouth wide open and his eyes shining like stars. Then he dropped his towel and took off like a rabbit shouting, "It's my Papa! It's my Papa!"

I didn't move. So, his father had recovered! I had come to share in this hope and in that prelude to his dreams, evening after evening, which rang so clear in the darkness of the dorm: "Tomorrow, when my father comes..." And my heart would sing in echo: "comes...comes...comes."

We were *so* longing for some newfound love. To dissolve ourselves into that "waiting for someone who would come" was as blissful as heaven. Jad's buzzing of hope was so intense that I forgot there was no place for me in that magic "will come." I listened to him and the orphanage's walls disappeared to let us run towards a little house with a red roof and green shutters. Our Mamas came to meet us. They took us in their arms, hugged us, kissed us. They said: "My soul, my house, my eyes, my heart, my life, my light, the war does not exist. It's only a nightmare that we must forget."

And we rediscovered their warmth which was unlike any other. Yes, in the softness of their hugs, war could not have existed.

"Tomorrow, when my father comes..."

He had come and the pain of it crushed my heart.

Sister Marie came to me: "Come on, Naseem, slip on your flannels and your socks or you will catch cold. A little bird told me that the sun is going to shine for you, too. Jad is very fond of you, you know. And so are we, Naseem. Do you hear me?"

I could hear her all right. What did she know of my sunshines? And what did I care if I caught cold? *He* had come. In a few months, a few weeks, perhaps a few days, *He* would take his son away. I myself was nobody's son anymore. *Nobody's*. Allah! Why the war, why, why, why?

I looked around me. Where could I run to hide and cry to my heart's content? In this world where I felt so alone, I could not find a corner where I could be alone, except under the shelter of my blankets at night. But at night, everything was so scary.

I was staring at the door through which Jad had left. I wished I could have smashed it with my fists and run away. Who cared if it would have been to another nowhere. I wanted to leave, to run away from this new pain, to die under the bombs.

The door opened and Jad dashed in. "Come on, quick. *He* wants to see you."

Oh Jad, Jad, my brother! He had left his long-awaited father to come and get me. I gave him a puzzled look. Impatiently, he dragged me by the hand. "Quick! Come on, hurry up! Oh, St. Elijah, what have I done to you that you have stuck this slug on me?"

We rushed down the stairs. Jad was exulting and I was in a daze. *He* stood up as we approached. *He* picked me up and held me at arm's length exactly as my father used to. My body and my soul shivered with nostalgia and gratitude. These strong hands around me. This feeling of being totally wrapped up in someone's tenderness.

He said, "So, here is my son's brother? Allah! he is just as handsome!"

Jad was hopping around us: "Papa, he's had a shock and he can't speak. I have explained it to you. Oh, Papa, my Papa!"

We found ourselves, both of us, in his lap. What they said

to each other, I did not hear. I felt like I was in a dream. He was my father and yet he was not. A strange feeling of well-being numbed my senses while at the same time, a voice whispered to me: "It's not true. *He* can't love you as his son. Nothing is true, except your family's death. One day they will both leave and you'll be left behind, shut in here for the rest of your life."

That night, it was Jad who cried, and I who got up to comfort him. Since I could not speak, I laid my head on his shoulder and wiped his tears with one of my pajama sleeves.

"I am thinking of Mama and Jihan," he said. "Papa and me, without them, you see, it's not even one half of life."

Not even one half of life? I don't know why, but this sentence stuck with me for a long time. What did we know of life, except that it was the opposite of death? And what did we know of death before the war—this death which had become a synonym for violence, hatred, shattered houses, torn and charred bodies, of rivers of blood? This death which took everything at once and left you alone with fear, despair, and a feeling of helplessness as paralyzing as a nightmare?

Not even half of life? Who said: "I have a whole life ahead of me," and opened her arms to welcome the immensity of her tomorrows?

I remember...

*   *   *

She was dancing in front of our mother because her birthday cake was rising in the oven, round and golden like a moon given to her in her dreams. Because in her sky there were only swallows. Because she believed in loving, giving, sharing. Because as she would blow out her seventeen candles, she would trigger a new round of tomorrows and forevers, which would dance to the infinity of her quest for happiness.

There she was, Lamia, our older sister, twirling away in the beauty of her seventeen Springs, of her clear laughter, of her trust in the durability of her tendernesses, of the sun that twinkled in her eyes and touched her cheeks with pink, of life itself, which she wanted to feel, to stroke, to knead and to model in her own way. Of her hymns to independence and of her sudden indignation: "Mama, when I think that at my age you were already married! By the way, why did you marry Papa rather than somebody else? And why so early?"

"Your father is not to your taste?" laughed Mama.

"Yes, yes, very much! People say of him: Put him on a wound and the wound will heal. It's true, he is kind. But at seventeen, one has a whole life ahead of oneself."

"And, according to my nightingale, what is life?" laughed Mama, who knew her daugher inside out.

A whole life ahead of oneself...

Lamia was capable of imagining anything, even dancing on the moon. Anything, that is, except war...and because of it, not a shadow of life would be left for her.

As for me, I naively and loudly proclaimed that when it came to parents, the girls in the family seemed to turn blind or stupid. Mama with someone other than Papa, or Papa with someone other than Mama? It was totally inconceivable. Besides, how could my parents ever have been anything but my parents all their life? This was at least what I believed until they explained to me that they had chosen each other, and that this was how families began.

Now, I was the one who wanted to know. I longed for the slightest detail. I regretted that their union had seemed so obvious that I had neglected to ask any questions.

Yet, I knew much more than I was aware of. The history of my family's birth lay entangled in the jumble of my memories. I was not trying to put them in order, but, as my mind mulled time and again over what had been my life in our village, memories of each and every one of them became linked together to form a whole which I would read and reread within myself and find more enchanting than a fairy tale.

And this is why, much later, I was able to tell you this story, Jad, because you knew my need to talk about them and call them by their names, and you were listening with your motherly heart.

11

Once upon a time, then, there were Najm and Saida, my father and my mother.

At age twenty—may Allah grant you a long life!—Najm was tall, handsome and suntanned with curls like an Eastern archangel.

People praised his cajoling smile, the honey of his friendship, his generous hand, his sunny disposition, the ease with which he seemed to live, his willingness to help, his earnestness at work, and his skillfulness. Truly, he was all that "and a half"—as full of qualities as he was of weaknesses, with such charm that everyone ate out of his hand.

Everyone, that is, except Saida, whose braids he had pulled a little too often when they were children. She made no bones about flinging at him, in outrageously sarcastic terms, what she thought of him, in general, and of his luck at playing marbles, in particular.

True, he was lucky at everything, and the marbles of Saida's brother Tannoos somehow always ended up rattling in Najm's pockets. But, to swear upon the cross that he cheated...well, that was something else, and Saida should have run to confession for daring to tell such shocking lies!

Tannoos was neither dexterous nor resourceful, and his sister defended him on principle for the sake of fraternal solidarity, for the pleasure of standing up to someone stronger than she was, or for any other obscure motive. How would you know with a girl who "had all her teeth against you"! And she was not one to mince her words or to kick half-heartedly either! In fact, besides a vocabulary thorny as the devil, she possessed a very personal and diverse kicking technique which was the envy of more than a few boys.

With the rest of the human race she was sweeter and more mellow than a vanilla sherbet. And at sixteen—may Allah prolong your years!—she was so exquisite, so radiant, so cheerful, that there was a swarm of boys trying their hands at romantic zajals* in the hope of filling her ears and heart with admiration. Needless to say, Najm carefully avoided entering those contests and bragged about it so ostentatiously that Saida spread the rumor that this poor Najm had about as much poetic sense in him as a piece of wood. "What good could his beautiful dark eyes be if they did not glimmer like the waves in the moonlight, unrolling towards shores bristling with fragrant rhymes?" Najm griped. But now that he could no longer pull her braids, he would only shrug and cast her as haughty a glance as he could muster.

Saida was expecting her mother to "take her pulse" one of these days to find out what she thought of this or that young man in the village. But the truth was she thought nothing of anyone. Her heart was quietly idling away and would only beat faster—an indignant beat, upon her honor!—under the mocking look of that boorish Najm who was so stuck up he thought he was the eighth wonder of the world.

Then, one day, there returned to the village a family of emigrants who had left more than three hundred moons ago to hunt for prosperity beyond the sea and the ocean.

Rich—Abu Jeries and Emm Jeries had become rich indeed! But the more their pocketbook filled up, the more they missed their small country, their small mountain, their small house, their very old parents, their brothers,

---

*A kind of improvised, dialogued poetic jousting, rhythmic and rhymed, sung by two or more partners. In Lebanon, Zajal is the popular poetry.

sisters, uncles, aunts, cousins, nephews, nieces, friends and neighbors.

They talked about them with their hands over their hearts, as they lowered their eyelids on eyes brimming with visions of the faraway country; and their voices were like a lullaby rustling in the breeze of memories.

They told of what cannot be told: of a home which is like nowhere else, of feelings which sing, crackle, burst and flare up or become happy and silent memories, long and shimmering like a streak of moonlight.

They told of the mysterious link which binds people to their land and of the language beyond words which links the people of the same land. Of the colors and fragrances by which one's soul is elated. Of the togetherness of evenings, these intense moments of sharing when the tales, the listening, the dreams, and the laughter rise like the song of a flute in the supreme peace of the night.

They told of the pleasure there is in knowing one another and endlessly rediscovering one another, and meeting one another and gathering together, and telling of joys again and again so that they branch out into every home, and telling of pains again and again so that their weight and their tears are gently alleviated by this togetherness.

They reminisced so much that their children finally became homesick for their country, although they had never known it, and their eyes brimmed with visions of the faraway land as their voices, like lullabies, persuaded their friends that at home, over there, at the other end of the earth, in their little country which was all mountains and sea, nothing was like anywhere else.

Over there, people lived together all their lives from beginning to end. Over there, old age never meant loneliness and childhood never meant fear and uncertainty. A gesture, a word, a caress, a smile, an open door, a place at the table, someone listening at all times of the day and night...because living together meant being immersed into one thousand tendernesses, and tenderness was the sunshine of life.

One evening, the east wind blew in a different way, soft, fragrant, sunny. It blew like a poem, as if it came straight from that small country over there, at the other end of the world, from that small country where people lived together, where houses were intertwined, where parents called all children "my child."

It blew like a call.

That evening, Abu Jeries and his family could no longer bear to see the sun disappearing at the end of the plain that marked their horizon. They wanted the light-spangled sea at the foot of the mountains, the rose-colored clouds in the fading daylight and the horizon streaming with purple and gold.

They wanted the voices of the village, the morning calls and those of the evening, the waking up of the children in the love of the dawn of each sunrise, their cries, their laughter and their tears, and the hurts that a kiss will erase.

They wanted other people's children with their own children, ears of the same wheat planted in the same field, rocked by the same song, soaked in the same rain and the same prayer for a harvest of life, for an infinity of hope and love.

The wind blew as a reborn secret and they knew what they had always known, perhaps a little tarnished by time and distance. They knew that one is never more present than in the hands stretching out in the same gesture of offering and of welcome, of prayer, reunion and recognition, a gesture which opens one up infinitely.

That gesture was the daily bread on their little mountain where time had nothing to do with dates or with the accumulation of wealth and esteem. Hurry, hurry before illness, old age and death have a chance to overtake you!

Time was meant for living, and most of all for loving ...above all with the kind of love that turns any suffering and any joy into a self-surpassing new birth, into a sense of accomplished presence.

Abu Jeries and his family breathed in this sweet, fragrant, sunny east wind. Dizzy with nostalgia, they made the decision to go home to their small village and to get their first-born son, Jeries, married there.

On the other side of the Atlantic, he was known as George. He was twenty-three, tall and slim, and his face was that of a prince from the *Thousand and One Nights*, with large dark eyes full of dreams. He was rich, too, which was just as well!

Who in the village could have forgotten Abu Jeries except those who were mere tots when he had left and those who were born while he was away? At home, those who have left keep their place just as much as those who have stayed, and the former almost more than the latter because they are talked about so much all the time. Just because someone leaves is no reason to cross him out of your thoughts. Abu Jeries' letters and those of his wife made the rounds in the village. Everyone knew their life "out there" by heart. When each of their children was born, three boys and three girls (may Allah keep them in good health and under their parents' protection), their Tetas had baked lots of meghlehs*—one large dishful for each house. Their Jeddos had passed arak around. Everyone had drunk to their health and prayed that Allah make them return peacefully.

And when they came back, there was a crowd in the church square to greet them. Oh, my eyes, what a welcoming party! Unbelievable! And the bells, and the offerings of

---

*A sweet meat prepared traditionally at the birth of a child with rice flour, sugar, pistachios, pine nuts and almonds.

bread and salt, and the hugs, and the speeches, and the laughter and the tears. . . .

But first, Abu Jeries knelt down to kiss his home ground. Then he was offered some cool water from the spring. He drank for a long time, holding the jug at arm's length so that everyone could see he still had the knack of it. Then he entered the church to bow to his patron saint and tell him of the joy of his return.

As for Jeries, it was true he was handsome as the moon, but he looked as though he had just landed on it! Just think! Born on the other side of the world, where everyone lives for himself, where one hardly knows the names of his neighbors. He realized that hearing about something and seeing it with one's own eyes were not at all the same thing. Not at all! He opened wide his handsome, wistful eyes and when they fell upon Saida, they stopped there with such a dazzled look that everyone noticed it and rejoiced at the prospect of a beautiful wedding.

Everyone? Not quite! Who knows why, but just then Najm suddenly saw Saida through Jeries' eyes and made up his mind that he would show them all; he would not let it happen!

Surely, the heart's reasons have nothing to do with reason. And who knows why, just then, Saida blushed like a cloud at sunset, not because of Jeries, but because of Najm!

Abu Jeries and Emm Jeries first took time to follow the customs of the village. They visited the homes that had been stricken by death while they were away. They expressed the deep sorrow they had felt in spite of the distance, asked many questions, and lamented abundantly and sincerely before concluding that "Allah wanted it that way."

Then the village filed off into *their* house to welcome them all over again and tell them of how immense their joy was to see them again. Later they returned the visits, congratulated the betrothed, the newly-weds, the happy parents of newborns and so on.

Finally, they were free to come and go as they pleased and to "take Jeries' pulse" to find out whether the dazzled shock of the first day was only a mirage or a certainty in his heart. Alas, he liked Saida more and more, but there was no way to know what she thought of him. Never mind, they were going to start the usual procedure and see what would happen.

Emm Jeries talked to Abu Jeries, who talked to his older brother, who talked to I don't remember whom, who talked to the brother of Saida's father, who talked to his brother, who talked to his wife, who set out to sound her daughter's heart. Of course, nothing would be forced on her. She must not imagine that her very loving father was in a hurry to get rid of her. But why not think about it, since Jeries was young, handsome, honest and rich, which was just as well. And think of the travel, the ship, the sea, a new country, in-laws as kind and sweet as honey, a husband so sweet you would be a queen until your last breath. Just think! And your heart is not already taken, as far as I know!

But yes, her heart was taken. She did not understand how, it was truly a mystery to her. Her heart had played such a strange trick on her—melting for that boorish Najm, of all people, who seemed to be content with casting gloomy looks at her without saying a word. He did not even contradict her any more. Allah! how she missed it! And how was she to make a decision if he did not break his silence? This had been going on for a month already. Should she throw herself into Jeries' arms out of spite?

Najm was not speaking up for good reason—he was so deeply moved by the suddeness of his feelings that he could no longer tell the North from the South. Besides, he was not sure of Saida's feelings. And an evil genie whispered to him that, given a choice between travels and him, Saida might well choose to turn her back on him. Furthermore, they had always fought too much. And Jeries' proposal was almost official. It already was the talk of the whole village. And...

He could take it no longer and ran to confession and begged the parish priest, who knew the sins and minor faults of everyone, to come to his assistance. The priest smiled. There were few things that escaped him. He knew very well what to think of all this. He had christened, confirmed, and prepared these two imps for their first communion. He had heard their confession and reconciled them many times, and he knew that all along they had done nothing but love each other (braid-pulling and kicking included) without ever wanting to admit it. It had taken no less than seeing Saida about to be whisked from under his nose to finally open the eyes of that foolish Najm.

That very night, the priest went to spend the evening with Saida's parents. He accepted a glass of arak, asked about everybody's health, spoke of the weather and the sowing, of the children who "when they are small, step on their parents' toes and when they grow up, step on their hearts. Insh'Allah may they bury us!" Anyway, they grow up too fast and their parents only want their happiness, don't they, even when it might seem to go against reason, or to the detriment of certain seemingly enticing advantages. But who can tell! He also talked of the serious honest young men of the village and how he did not like one better than the others. No, they were all his children. But getting two children married when only one of them was in love would make the other one unhappy, which, of course, ended up making two people unhappy.

I don't know what he said to Jeries and his parents the next evening. His Sunday homily somewhat baffled the congregation. He preached in a jumble about self-sacrifice and generosity of heart, of patience, that splendid virtue which never fails to bear fruit, and the urgency of favoring what it was good to favor, since too long a wait might cause the best fruit to wither. To each ear, what it must hear!

Still, Najm was too young and his father thought, with good reason, that he needed to mature quite a bit before he could contemplate the responsibilities of a family.

"All right," advised the priest, who thought it would not take Saida very long to stabilize her husband. "Sigh as hard as you can when you're around your mother, Najm, and I guarantee that things will move fast."

Najm sighed. He looked out of sorts and lost his appetite. It took only one day. The very first evening, his mother became alarmed by her son's lack of vitality and feared the onset of a serious illness. She examined his pulse first, then his soul. Thank God, he had no fever or sickness whatsoever. He was only in love. (Insh'Allah, that he may bury her!) She was flabbergasted when she heard with whom. For heaven's sake, how could that be? Didn't he know that everybody knew she was as good as already married to Jeries?

"Let's see," the priest said when he was called upon for advice. "There is no church or civil law that prohibits two proposals, is there?"

So, the mother talked to the father, who talked to his brother, who talked to the priest, who talked directly to Saida's father, who talked to his wife, who sounded her daughter's heart and guessed the joy she would see in her eyes.

Jeries resigned himself and married someone less boisterous than Saida and better suited to his wistful eyes, and it is said that he lived very happily ever after.

12

My parents were happy together. Truly happy. And we were born from their happiness. I remember their wedding picture in the living room and, around it, the pictures of our christenings and first communions. If only I could have taken them with me! Were they left undamaged in the rubble of our house?

Since then, I have seen many more ruins. One detail upset me most: that of an undamaged toy next to the crushed body of a child. Just a few days ago, after a car-bomb explosion which wounded and killed many people, I saw a doll next to the broken body of a little girl. I picked it up. It was still warm with the warmth of the arms that had cuddled her. I wished I could have given it the breath of the departed child, and the child's dream of a happiness without threat. It seemed to me its hazel-colored eyes with movable lids reflected the little girl's last adoring look and her tender, loving words.

Blinded by tears, I put the unharmed doll down next to the child whose arms were folded across her face in a piteous, useless gesture of protection. An instant before, she had been smiling, infinitely alive, infinitely loving, like a morning glory turned up to drink from the sky, with its bloom shaped for the day's offerings, and plump, full of life—of her life which she believed would last till the end of life itself...full of the love which a child is so good at giving and receiving totally.

Why did she have to be broken and leave us? Why were her promises undone? Why had she been torn to pieces by hatred?

My father, my mother, I have learned how to bring first

aid to the injured, to encourage, to console, to delicately lift up a stretcher to spare the victim any painful jolt, to run towards an ambulance holding a small limp body with perhaps a little bit of life left in it. In front of a child in agony I recall your words and your gestures in order to find my way to the core of his or her terror. I make a cradle of my arms, putting in that gesture all the gentleness in the world—yours, my mother, when you would rock me when I was feverish, with your song rising in the shadowy light of sunset like the perfume of incense in a sanctuary.

Your song, Mama, how could I ever forget it? I have heard it so often in the shelters, a thousand times multiplied on the lips of a thousand mothers. I have sung it myself, too, to children without a mother, and your face was there, with the lively melody and your voice to chase away the terror—gentle, so gentle in the thundering sound of death, rising in a twirl of prayer, hope and certainty:

> O Lallaa, my child, may Allah look after him,
> O Lallaa, may all the angels in heaven look after him.
> My child is the moon, my child is the dawn,
> My child is more beautiful than the most beautiful pearl
>   on earth.

This was your lullaby, Mama, and it danced on your lips, your song of praise and prayer for those "whom your heart had seen long before your eyes saw them."

> O Lallaa, may he fall asleep, my little one,
> O Lallaa, may sleep come to him.
> O Lallaa, may he love prayer and love the Virgin.

I am listening to you, Mama, and my prayer rises from the depth of my childhood and of all the childhoods I have seen being rocked in the shelters. I sing like you, Mama, and like all the mothers who hold back their tears to calm the fear in their little ones:

Sleep, O my eyes,
Basil of my garden,
May Allah protect you from all evils,
Now and forever.
Listen, your father is praying.
Listen, your mother is praying.
We are all in Allah's hand,
What is there to fear?
Sleep, O my eyes, basil of my garden.

And when the thunder of death recedes in the first glimmer of dawn, I pray, Mama, for all the broken children of this mad earth. I pray, and again I listen to you, Mama, you whose song was all vigor and prayer. You said, hugging us, "Ah, will I ever manage to teach you all the tenderness that prays inside me?"

Yes, Mama, you taught us all the tenderness that was praying inside you. You taught us to see, to touch, to listen to life. You taught us that nothing was more beautiful, more fabulous, more important, more essential than to love. And Papa taught us with you.

But neither you nor he have taught me how to keep from crying in front of the nameless horror. Nor how to ask for whom, for what, people were being killed in that way. Nor how to stuff the remains of a human being into a plastic bag without shivering with all my soul. Nor how to understand war.

I don't understand. I will never understand the war.

My father, my mother, where is she now, this child with the unbroken doll? Where is she joining her hands in a never-ending prayer? She had the same hollow look of horror in her eyes as my sister Hala on the day when... I closed her lids down onto her blind eyes—the gesture I had not been able to do for you, my family, because, then, I didn't know how.

What a strange feeling to close forever the eyes of a little being, as if to complete her departure from this earth. I like to think that she has found again the light of her eyes up there, in the endless light, near someone who calls her "light of my heart, my eyes, my house, my soul, my life." Because that is what remains, Mama, this nourishing well-spring of song which nothing can erase, because truly, without love, there is no soul.

My father, my mother, are they alive, those who kill and those who make weapons? Have they ever curved their arms to cradle a life and arouse its soul by calling it "my soul"? Don't they know that in such an embrace everything is resolved, and opens up, and is born and reborn, and is multiplied to infinity? Don't they know it is by thinking of himself as the home of those he loves that a child will learn he can become a home for all, built to welcome, to give away his harvests in abundance, to give warmth and leave the door open, to give everyone a chance to take off in their flight towards the essential.

My father, my mother, I wish I could have painted and drawn in colors of light what cannot be put into words. I wish I could have played the flute and expressed the inexpressible with trills. I wish I could have been a poet and rhymed what cannot be told in rhythms of light. Because when you called me your soul, with your loving gaze, the warmth of your loving arms, the clarity of your loving words, with your hands joining mine for a loving prayer, you made me become light for the eternity of each of my heartbeats. When you called me your house, you made me become a house open for the whole earth. In this house, the war will never enter.

*   *   *

Christmas was coming. A fresh outbreak of violence added to the sadness of our exile. There was gunfire all over the place. Under these conditions, Christmas seemed even more remote and elusive than a star.

Eager to feel some of the happiness of old times, we snuggled more deeply into our memories. In the yard, Jad gave up his games. He would sit next to me and swing his legs for a long time before starting his monologues.

"I hate the war," he said in a muffled voice. "It's what I hate the most in all the world.

"Why don't we have Mamas anymore? Why are we here? Why do we have to be afraid all the time? Can you hear the gunfire? It doesn't sound like a holiday's coming.

"At home, every evening before Christmas, before we went to bed, Mama turned off all the lights in the house except the ones of the manger and the tree. They blinked on and off, on and off, one after the other, and it looked like they were running around the tree. And the light of the manger, it is always nicer than all the others, don't you think? It looks different from all the others.

"Say, do you believe in Santa Claus? Me, I stopped believing ages ago.

"We used to plant grains of wheat and lentils. They grew so beautifully. And we had lots of prayers and songs. Mama would take me in her lap and she would say: 'Sing with me, my soul.' I sang a little and then I would stop, just to listen to her, because, I must tell you, Mama had the most beautiful voice in the world. She did, I swear it. Even Papa used to say so!"

Jad abruptly stopped talking, his lips trembling. Like me, he didn't want to cry in front of the others. I think he hated as much as I did to be asked, "Why are you crying?" which one can't answer when the pain suffocates you.

My Mama too had the most beautiful voice in the world. My Papa too swore to it: "Upon my honor, my wife, you sound like an angel." When he had married Saida, Najm had discovered he had the soul of a poet.

I too had stopped believing in Santa Claus ages ago. With the war, I hardly even believed in Christmas anymore.

While Jad swallowed back his tears, we looked at the sky.

The sky of an orphanage's yard is cut off from the rest of the earth, a bit of sky without any mountains or sea. Some sad, grey clouds slowly drifted by as if they had lost their way.

When it was raining, we stood under an awning. Our sadness followed us there, more dense and stifling than the outdoors. I felt like I was suffocating. Jad would take my hand.

"If only you could speak. I would like to know the color of your voice. If only you could at least nod yes or no when I ask you questions. Here, I have an idea. Write me something so that I'll know at least if you have any thoughts. I am answering everybody in your place and I don't even know if what I say is the truth. Naseem, I swear that you are my brother. Not just a make-believe brother. A real one. And you are my best friend. Only, it's tiring, a friend who doesn't even blink to let me know he can hear me. Oh, St. Elijah, when will it come, that shock that will make you speak? Don't you even want to tell me if I am your best friend?"

How sweet were these words, dedicated to me. Here I was, receiving everything from my Jad without giving him anything back. Paralyzed by my dumbness, I had forgotten that signs too could be an approach, a link, a language. I shook my head for a frantic "Yes," thus releasing my silence from its solitude.

Jad's panicked hand stopped me: "Stop it, or you're going to dislocate your head! All the same, I'm happy. Say, it's the first time I've seen you smile. And when you smile, what can I say? You are the handsomest brother in the world!"

13

When Jad was called to the parlor for the second time, like the first time, I didn't move. Overjoyed, he dashed away. I knew, somehow, that he would return as fast as he had left. He did reappear like a tornado: "You know what Papa said? He said: 'What is this, you're coming alone? Where is your brother Naseem?' Hurry up...Oh, Allah, you're so slow! Hurry, he's waiting."

I wasn't as quick or impatient as Jad in the face of his joys. In fact, I didn't really believe all this. A whispering voice inside me repeated endlessly: "He is waiting for *us* today. But tomorrow, when they leave for good, it will just be the two of them. And I will die. I will die for sure."

Like the first time, Jad's father rose to his feet as we came in the room, and I threw myself into his arms. At that minute, I realized that I had been waiting for him as intensely as his son. I loved this father with as much love as Jad had for him.

He held my face in his hands. I stared at him with an immense longing in my eyes. I wanted him to say: "You are mine!" Oh, Allah! How I wanted to belong to him for good. Forever. To be sure he would not take Jad away from me.

He said nothing. He pulled two tiny cars out of his pocket and handed them to us with a smile. My hand was shaking when I took mine. A present. A present for me! He had thought of both of us when he had bought them. Of both of us together. Of Jad and Naseem. So, I really existed for him, even outside of this parlor!

I stared at him with new eyes. He loved me. At that minute, I knew it for sure. His smile told me so. His hand on my hair told me so. His present in my hand told me so.

They loved me. He and Jad loved me! That was immense.

I had begun to exist again. It was a little bit of my village coming back to me. It was all that mattered for the time being.

*   *   *

Christmas was now only three days away. Unconsciously, I was waiting for the war to disappear. Christmas and the war didn't seem to go together at all.

The war meant blasts, death, the end of happiness and of holidays, darkness and fear.

Christmas was meant to be all stars, mangers, songs, fires sparkling everywhere. I felt that a secret and all-pervasive gentleness took over heaven and earth to make them more intensely real so that what my parents used to call "the immensity of a gift of love" could come to pass.

At home, Papa and Yussef took care of the tree while Mama and Lamia opened up the large box where our manger was kept. They took out the figures cautiously. One by one they emerged from the straw, marvelous and mysterious, inviting meditation just as much as the year before. Yes, even the ox, the ass, and the sheep. Milad, Hala and I stared at them in silence, overcome by a happiness equally mysterious and meditative.

As I ecstatically looked at them all spread out on the table, it seemed to me that, under our eyes, the figures of our nativity set unfolded and unfurled their story anew as they made their way into the manger. Then we would disentangle the angel's hair, so light in our fingers that it felt as though we'd been touching the stars.

The next day, Mama baked all sorts of cakes and mountains of cookies shaped like stars, crescent moons, Christmas trees, snowmen and flowers. She baked them for us, for our family, our guests, our neighbors and our friends. The whole house smelled deliciously of vanilla and syrup—

a delicious fragrance which seemed to carry with it all kinds of impressions and happy memories.

When he came back at night, Papa would exclaim: "How good Christmas smells at home! May God keep you all in peace." And Mama replied: "May God keep you above our heads, you, the pillar of our house, and may He open all the hearts on earth."

No, Christmas with the war was not possible. Yet, to someone who had seen a village all crushed within a few hours, anything could seem possible. Anyway, at the orphanage, one did not "feel" Christmas the way one did at home.

                    *   *   *

Suddenly, I remembered Mama's orange blossoms and began to sniff like a puppy following a scent.

"Don't you have a handkerchief?" asked Jad. "Here, take mine. Here comes Ramzi, to sit with us. Let's make room for him."

I moved up a little and the three of us swung our legs rhythmically. Ramzi seemed uncharacteristically lost in thought. He cast a sidelong glance at Jad and embarked on one of his usual speeches: "The day after tomorrow, I'll go home for the holiday. My Mama will give me a roomful of toys and my Papa . . ." Jad nudged me as if to say: "You see, it's always the same thing!"

But we did not feel like laughing. Ramzi's sadness was as thick as ours, and so much more desperate.

"Yes," said Jad to comfort him. "Yes, sure. One day, things will finally happen the way we want them to. But sometimes it takes a while. Sure, your parents love you, Ramzi. It's not their fault if they have problems. But just think! They are still alive!"

That same day, during study, Sister Marie came to find Jad. I thought she must need him to help her move the chapel benches in order to clean up for the celebration. For once, I did not mind his being away. I wanted to give him a big drawing with a letter for a Christmas present, a project I could not undertake in his presence.

I had never done any drawing at the orphanage so far, so I imagined how surprised and happy this was going to make him.

First of all, I unfolded his drawing which I kept with the greatest care and looked at it to draw inspiration from it. Then I took out his father's small car which was parked in my pocket. With my two treasures in sight I suddenly panicked. I saw myself alone with those mementoes when Jad left with his father. Christmas or not, whether the war ended or not, there was no place for me anywhere except in this orphanage.

Allah! how I suddenly needed to see real landscapes and to run freely on open roads. Allah! how I longed to throw myself into my mother's arms. To say "Mama" once, only once, and feel the gentle coolness of her hand on my burning forehead. To hear her voice again, once, only once more, calling me "her life," and then to die, because without her, the world was horribly empty. She had been my rock, my permanence, my trust, my lamp when the earth ushered in the night, and my sun of every season. She had been my Christmas every day, my everything, and now she was gone. Allah! how cold I felt. Alive, she would never have left me. What was I for Jad, himself another mother-less little boy who did not want to leave me, but could not decide his own fate anymore than I could? What was I for his father, whom I loved, but who was going to leave me here, stuck inside the walls of this orphanage forever?

I fought as hard as I could against the black tide which was once again engulfing me. I didn't want to cry in the middle of study. Also, I had to make a drawing for Jad. Near me or far away, he had opened a new dawn for me. It wasn't his fault if it had to close up again.

I drew a garden with multicolored flowers and a huge sun in a cloudless sky. I wrote: "To Jad, from his friend Naseem, a Christmas present." Then I set out to write my letter. I concentrated hard, trying to correct my mistakes, but it soon became apparent that this was impossible. At seven, hesitating over the spelling of a word is more of a torture than the endeavor itself. How could any kind of speculation shed light on what one simply doesn't know? I gave up and let my pen run freely: "To my friend Jad, I wish you a Merry Christmas with your Papa. He is tall, he is handsome, he is nice. I like him very much because he is your Papa and you will be happy together, and I, I will be happy for that. Jad, don't ever forget me because I will never forget you. Your friend, from now until we die, Naseem."

I carefully folded my two sheets of paper and slipped them into the pocket of my smock. The bell rang before Jad got back.

It was drizzling and I went out to the sheltered part of the yard. I paced back and forth three times. No trace of Jad. Why was he away for such a long time? Could it be...? Oh God, no...not that, I beg you, not *that*! Could it be that his father had taken him away for the holiday? He couldn't have left without seeing me one last time.

I walked out into the yard. I wanted to be alone on our bench, far from the shouts and the games of the others. I offered my face to the icy-cold December drizzle. I heard a bell ringing in the distance. Its sound was soft and light, so much like the call of our bell at home. So, beyond the walls of the orphanage, were there still villages, houses, people who lived the way we used to? I had been so imprisoned in my own distress that I had forgotten it. For me, the only outside reality was war.

I listened to the merry ringing of the bell. It carried me from hill to hill and dropped me in our little church, in front of the manger, between Milad and Hala, my brother and sister. I touched the brown paper speckled with russet spots. I gazed at the inside of the small houses where the little lamps created a mysterious light. I love the light in the grotto. Jad was right to say it was incomparable. Far inside, Mary, Joseph, the ass, the ox and the straw in the manger all seemed to be waiting for the arrival of Jesus at the midnight Mass. I wished I could have become a shepherd and knelt there, in this peaceful light which seemed to send forth hope to the whole world.

The shrill sound of the orphanage's bell brought me back into the hostile night, soaked in the drizzle. I felt so weak and distressed that I couldn't move. What did I care about the cold, the rain and Christmas, as long as I didn't belong to anyone? I might as well sink into the night, not to think anymore, not to remember, what a relief!

The small bell in the distance stopped abruptly. Then the bombs took over. They brought death from hill to hill. Were they coming back to our blackened village on Christmas eve where, in the old days, presents, good wishes and prayers would have begun to be shared all around?

"I'm bringing you your share of sweets, my neighbors! Double health and happiness to you. May you celebrate until you are a hundred years old and may each year find you in peace!"

To celebrate Christmas in my village. To pray in Mama's lap. Through our joined hands, to feel heaven opening up in a cascade of angels and songs: "Glory to God in the highest, and peace on earth to men of good will."

Peace on earth. I heard Mama's voice: "Peace, light of my heart, is love and the respect of life."

Peace, my tender Mama? Could you hear the bombs from up there in heaven? Right this minute, more families were being annihilated. Right this minute, other children were dying to life, dying to tenderness. My Christmas was peopled with dismembered or charred bodies like those I had seen at the village, those I saw on television, those I heard of and those who were falling right now, while the world was getting ready to sing of the opening of heaven.

My Christmas was peopled by the dead. I slumped on my bench and I begged heaven to give me back my mother.

Once more I woke up in the infirmary. Sister Marie dried me, wrapped me inside a large, warm towel, and made me swallow a lump of sugar dipped in brandy. In spite of all this, I kept shivering with cold and weariness. Jad shook me as if he wanted to finish drying me.

"Oh, St. Elijah, when will you stop scaring us? Everytime, I think you're dead. And couldn't you have picked another day? Today of all days, you mustn't die, not today."

He was shouting, but as he was hammering away his "todays," his face was lit up with intense joy. He seemed to have found a new happiness so great that he was temporarily losing his mind. He turned to Sister Marie: "Please tell him, tell him he must be happy today, even if he doesn't know why."

"Shh!" said Sister Marie. "You love Naseem, don't you?"

She emphasized the word "love." I got the impression that she meant something I must not understand. But Jad understood and said: "Oh, yes!" and calmed down at once.

Much later, I discovered his father had come that day. He had a long talk with the Mother Superior and with Sister Marie before asking for Jad. He was coming to give him the only present his little boy asked for insistently, but he was asking him to be patient just a little while longer because, in order to be permanent, this very peculiar present demanded a lot of formalities.

To this day, I still marvel at the love of this father who could have taken his child away with him on Christmas eve. Most of all, I admire his child's acceptance and his silence as he resisted his overwhelming urge to sing his joy to me. "You see," he explained to me much later, "your recovery was at stake."

Once we were alone, I went and took my presents out of my smock pocket. They were soaked but still visible and legible. Jad unfolded them with care and said he had never received anything so beautiful (he must have been exaggerating!), and set them out on the bedspread to dry.

*   *   *

On Christmas day, Jad's father came to see us with two big soccer balls, two small bags full of balloons, and two bags of caramels. We had already been given presents from the orphanage: games, candies, and books. But nothing could compare with what had been thought of, bought, touched by *him*!

He would have liked to have taken us out for a long walk, but with the bombs, it would not have been wise. We had to be content with a short stroll outside. The weather was nice. I was surprised to find ourselves at the bottom of a valley. Where was the sea? I breathed in the air with delight. Allah! the mountains were so beautiful, strewn with small villages.

He walked slowly, holding us by our hands, with Jad on one side and me on the other. He bent down the way my father used to:

"So Naseem, are you happy to go out a little?"

"Yes, Papa," said Jad. "He's very happy and likes his new soccer ball. See how he's hanging onto your arm?"

Jad was clinging to his father the same way, but I made no comment. I was content to smile and nod my head.

"Wouldn't you two like to run around and play together?" he asked.

"No, Papa," Jad said. "For all the time I've known him, he has never run or played. Say, do you think that when . . . you know . . . when . . . do you think . . . ?"

"Yes," he answered. "Yes, I am sure."

We walked in silence. I did not attempt to see through Jad's hesitations. My Christmas was beautiful after all. It gave me that big hand for my first outing. A daddy's big hand, both gentle and strong, and so reassuring. I brought my face closer to it. With my eyes closed, I could almost believe it was my father's.

Jad suddenly said: "You know, Papa, the day before yesterday, he wanted to die in the rain. Tell him we don't want him to die. Tell him something!"

Had I really wanted to die? I wasn't sure anymore. After all, life or death, they were so much alike sometimes. One died so many times with the war. I had died with my family. I died of fright with my nightly ghosts. I would die when Jad left.

But there were times like this morning when one felt exquisitely born anew, when people around you became real again.

He squeezed my hand. I lifted my head and met his gaze—my Papa's gaze when he called me his soul.

"Naseem, my soul," he said, "I love you very much. Jad and I, we love you forever."

That was life. Undoubtedly. How bright was the sun that morning!

14

The second term went by, slow and uneventful. Jad was changing every day. He studied with great earnestness, but his thoughts were clearly somewhere else. He never again said: "Tomorrow, when my father comes..." I know now that he was afraid of betraying himself. Where did this talkative little boy who couldn't hide any of his impulses find the strength to remain silent?

Deprived of his dreams for the future, and having none of my own, I sank a little further into the past. I relived every second of my life with my family. But there, too, time and absence dug impassable chasms. We were no longer "together." They were on one side, I was on the other. My memories had become the instruments of infinite separation.

Sometimes I prayed. The Sisters had given me a white rosary. I rolled it around in my fingers the way my parents used to. Strangely enough, in those moments, I felt again a real presence by my side. I did not doubt God's existence, even if I did not feel his kindness. I did not blame him for the war or for the death of my family. Was I too young for this kind of revolt? God had been given to me by my parents. Their tender love had anchored inside me the conviction of his tenderness. How can one understand divine love, invisible and silent, if not through an earthly love, touching and touchable, speaking and spoken to, which makes you brim over with joy and sunshine? If my parents were all love, God must be all love. If my parents rejected the war, God could not possibly have wanted it.

Only, I hadn't learned yet to differentiate between a visible presence and an abstract one. All this was rather confusing in my young mind. And, just as I kept talking to my absent parents, it seemed to me I also prayed to an absent God. They were all in heaven, I had no doubt. But to imagine heaven where the members of my family must be moving around without their bodies and without me— that was too much for me to comprehend. With them gone from the earth, so was God. And because heaven had deserted my heart, whatever might be going on up there, above the clouds, became incomprehensible.

With the coming of Spring, I was again expecting the end of the war. Even today, have we given up hope? Don't we hope without understanding why we are dying? At each lull in the fighting, we believe that peace has finally returned while, in fact, it is war which is gathering new strength to pounce on us again—more ferocious, more complex, more murderous than ever. Today, it seems this war's only purpose is to kill as many people as possible, just for the sake of killing, and as horribly as possible. And still we keep hoping.

I often think of the broken little girl lying next to her unbroken doll. She was born in the midst of the war, lived through the war, died because of the war. How could she imagine what peace might be like? What sense did this word of light make to her?

"What's a country at peace like?" asked a six year-old boy during a mad night of bombings.

Jad and I were lucky enough to have known what it was like. But this little boy, would he ever get a chance to find out?

"Would you like to go far away from here?" asked Jad.

"Go where?"

"To a country without war."

"Would we sleep every night in our beds?"

"Yes."

"Would we never be scared again?"

"No."

"We wouldn't see scary dead people all the time?"

"No."

"We could play outside without being scared?"

"Yes."

"But, that other country, it wouldn't be Lebanon?"

"No."

"Then I'd rather stay here."

"But here, there are the bombs."

"Yes, but even with the bombs, it's Lebanon. My Papa says it's our land and if all its sons leave it, it will die for good. I don't want our land to die."

"And what will you do when you grow up?"

"How can I tell you. We don't even know if we'll go to school tomorrow. You, what do you do? And your brother, what does he do?"

"We are learning to become rescue workers."

"What is that?"

Jad explained it to him, and it reminded me of his child-hood promise: "Tomorrow, when I grow up, I will do any kind of work against the war. Do you think that exists? Anyway, we'll do it together."

"Are you going to drive an ambulance?" asked the little boy with great interest.

"Maybe," said Jad, "but that's not what matters."

"What matters, then?"

"To love is what matters," said Jad who can speak so simply, so beautifully about such things.

"Ah! If I live, I will become a rescue worker, too," stated our little man clapping his hands. "I like to love."

"I like to bomb things," Ramzi used to shout defiantly. "Here I am, the pilot of a bomber plane. Bang! Bang! Bang! You're all dead!"

"Aren't you scared of bombshells?" asked Jad one evening when they were falling by the hundreds, not far from the orphanage.

"Yes, I am," Ramzi admitted, "but, you see, it's not the same thing being the one who aims and being the one who gets it. The one who aims is all-powerful. He can go where he pleases and do what he pleases. Nobody would dare to prevent him. Don't you think it's great?"

"No, I wouldn't like to go where I please and do what I please that way." And he added, full of misgivings, "And while you're at it, you wouldn't also torture people, would you?"

"Oh, no!" Ramzi protested, for in spite of it all, he was still a very sensitive child and wanted to destroy only in bulk and in abstract. "It's better to attack from far away. That way, you don't know and you don't see whom you have killed."

"It's killing all the same," Jad said. "And what do you want to attack for, anyway?"

"To be the strongest. Always the strongest. Wouldn't you like it too?"

"No, I don't like it at all."

"What do you like, then?"

"I like to love. All my life, I will like to love."

"You're stupid. It's useless."

"No, it isn't. My parents have always told me that it could lead to everything."

"Your Mama, what good did it do her? She's dead."

"You can say what you want," Jad concluded in a voice shaking with indignation and sorrow. "I can't explain it, but *I know*. It's something in here (he was pressing his hand on his heart), with my Mama."

*   *   *

Ramzi was seeking us out more and more. Was it because he felt we were really listening to him? He thoroughly enjoyed describing his parents to us, the way he wished them to be. In us, he found two pairs of attentive ears whose owners wouldn't even think of contradicting him. Jad always greeted him kindly and multiplied his

"Sure, Ramsi"s with the conciliatory airs of an adult talking to a child. I did not tolerate him as well because his questions too often hit me like punches in the stomach. He did not do it on purpose. He was struggling to understand so many things, this little boy at loose ends. To be eight-and-a-half with the world closed around him. Closed by the war and by his parents' problems. Closed ever since he was born.

"Why do you like Naseem more than the others?" he would ask Jad. "Why is he your best friend?"

"Because he doesn't have anybody left. Can't you see, he's lost everything, even his voice!"

"And when you go, what will he do?"

"I'm not leaving yet," Jad replied quickly, blushing to a cherry color while I felt on the verge of fainting. "I won't leave him. Oh, forget it, let's go play. Sometimes we talk too much."

But Ramzi was persistent. He turned to me and asked flatly: "How does it feel to be a double orphan? Who will ever get you out of here if you don't have anybody? You'd better make up your mind and run away. I will, as soon as my parents have a home together and..."

"Leave him alone," Jad blew up. "You can attack me as much as you please, but him, leave him alone. It's not fair, he can't answer you back."

Run away? Why not? I had already given it some thought. But where would I go with no one in the world to turn to. And how would I ever manage to escape the nights and their ghosts? Another child had run away the month before but he had soon been brought back. The hope for something else must be so overwhelming to launch you into the unknown like that. Or the lack of hope, perhaps? But I knew one could die wherever one happened to be. No need to wander anywhere else.

"Your soccer ball is beautiful," Ramzi said. "Too bad no one plays with it."

My ball and my miniature car. All my belongings in this world. Play with them? But these weren't *toys*, they were two *thoughts* from Jad's father. Two tangible links of love which I carefully kept at all times in my pocket and under my arm to be sure to preserve their permanence. The slightest scratch would have made them evaporate. Jad could shoot, scratch or even puncture his ball because of his certainty—it wouldn't have mattered. He had all of his father to himself. He had all of me, too. But I was probably only part of his kindness and not of his needs. I was only a parenthesis, not indispensable to his happiness.

Ramzi was casting such covetous glances on my ball that I felt moved. How many times had he been called to the parlor since Christmas? Twice, that was all. And he had come back with his fists tight inside his pockets—empty. He who talked so much of toys by the dozen. Both times he had cried and called in his sleep.

"You've had sweets, don't forget," Jad said consolingly.

"They don't last. Once you've eaten them, what's left? Nothing. You can't play with candies."

My heart sank with compassion. If I lent him my ball, I would still have my car. There are irresistible impulses like that which will remain forever unexplained. I handed my treasure to him.

"You mean you're lending it to me?"

I nodded my head, Yes.

"What if it gets damaged?"

So what, I shrugged my shoulders.

"May I . . . may I sleep with it one night?"

Yes, I nodded my head.

"But I'm not even your friend! For you, only Jad counts!"

Ah, said my heart.

Jad would lend his ball to anybody. Jad was ready to be everybody's friend. Why shouldn't I emulate him, I, his *best friend*. A wave of pride swelled my heart.

Here! said my hands, holding it out.

I gently threw my precious treasure. Ramzi caught it and said, "I'll be careful, cross my heart. I will return it to you almost as good as new. And...and...I'll never forget this, for the rest of my life!"

15

Spring seemed so fragile and bare. A brand new square of blue sky where brand new tufts of clouds swept by. A tree adorned with tender buds, lonely prisoner in its narrow circle of soil at the center of a yard made of concrete. It wasn't much. It wasn't enough!

Bare trees, flowering trees, trees bearing fruit or leaves —they were all so free, our trees at home. They drank from the winter rains or from the deep blue days speckled with honey-colored sunshine. Their branches swung in the wind in a dance which celebrated the rising of their sap, and their shadows, spotted with light, rustled under our steps like a purring, stretching happiness.

Ah! To scratch the bark of a pine tree, softly rugged under our palms, and stir up its reddish fragrance. To drink from the spring which spurts from the depths of the earth and picks up its nuances from the rays of the sun. To lie down in the grass alive with bugs and to close one's eyes to better capture the mysterious harmony of shade and light. And the flowers, everywhere, unrolling their colors in a miracle of airy grace: the daisies from which Lamia used to pluck the white petals "...Loves me, loves me not," the cyclamens in the rocky hollows in every shade from pink to carmine, the minute crystal bowls of the Venus' mirrors, the cheerful blue forget-me-nots, the bluebells quivering like a moth's wings, the hyacinths the color of the sea at sunset...Mama's sumptuous bouquets and ours, dishevelled as cascading petals.

A single tree adorned with tender buds at the center of a courtyard...that was so little, but so beautiful! It attracted birds and made our square of sky sing again. It brought back to me visions of the flowers from home: flowers flying like a balmy breeze, flowers singing a song as furtive as a sparrow's. How very beautiful our mountain was, the source of so many raptures! I closed my hands around the memories of our bouquets of the past—my hands which sufferings and loss were patiently initiating into the transparency of things. The flowers of bygone days trembled in my hands. I brought them close to my face and breathed in the story of the single Spring they spent next to century-old trees. A single Spring to become forever part of the surging fullness of life, and to accomplish their destiny.

"What are you holding?" asked Ramzi. "Nothing? What are you breathing? Nothing?"

"No," said Jad, with a sudden far-away look and his voice like a whispering brook. "No, he is holding the Spring of his village."

"So what," said Ramzi, who was a city boy who only enjoyed the nostalgia of honking horns and blinking neon lights. "So what. In the city, we have better things than the Spring."

"Ah! And how do you celebrate Palm Sunday without flowers?"

"We celebrate with candles, flowers and olive boughs which have been blessed the year before. Then we take the new ones."

"And do you have processions?"

"Of course, around the church."

"It's like in our villages, then?"

"Why wouldn't it be like your villages?"

"Does your father carry you on his shoulders for the procession?"

"Why wouldn't he? He buys a candle bigger than I am. Next Sunday, he will come to get me for the holiday. I'll tell you all about it."

"And the church, what's it like?"

"Like all churches."

"Not like ours, anyway."

"Why?"

"Ours is special because...because it's ours, that's why!"

"But it's been destroyed," said Ramzi surprised.

"So what, it's still special. And when we build it again, we'll build it special all the same."

"And Naseem's church?"

I didn't listen to the answer. I was brutally overcome by the thought that collapsed houses and churches could be rebuilt, but not collapsed families.

What colors were Jad's memories? He had been spared the sight of his crushed family. His dreams could keep the radiance of happy days and the gestures, the voice, the gaze, the hands and the face of his mother, unscathed and alive. Between his memories and himself, death had not edged in its horrible slaughter. He had not touched death. He did not know that a silenced hand can be as unbearable as a silenced voice, and that the terrible vision of your house and your loved ones shattered to pieces can make you feel equally shattered.

Noisy and enthusiastic, Ramzi and Jad were describing their respective processions to each other and marveled at finding they were so much alike in spite of the difference in the words they chose to describe them. Ramzi spoke of the price of candles, of his new suit, of the number of people at the Mass, of the many pounds of sweets his father would buy. How strange was that need of his to define things by their cost, their weight, or the time they would last. Did he hope to make them more real that way? Jad reminisced about the altar covered with flowers, Jihan's tiny hand irresistibly drawn to the small dancing flames, the long white line of choir boys and the wave of "hosannas," cheerful, triumphant, and iridescent like a cascade of sunshine.

It was true that our faith was all laughter, songs, flowers, tears, lights, silences, meditations, fervor, feasts and celebrations...always feelings, sensations, emotions, joy. Because what can't be put into words can be felt with our hearts, because brotherhood is made of linked hands, because it is with our lips that we can sing "alleluia" and with our eyes that we can live in colors.

Our Palm Sunday was so merry. With new clothes on, holding tall, fluted candles adorned with flowers and olive branches tied with ribbons, the children seemed to be ushering in the Spring.

On the steps of the sanctuary, the priest stood smiling, radiant and new like us in his crisp white surplice. His voice called cheerfully: "Let the children come to Jesus the way they come to those they love—running, singing, laughing, talking. Let them come in their own way." And we ran, and we laughed, free, free, flying because nothing is more splendid, more immense, more pervaded with God's grace and presence than to spring forward freely toward Love.

That Love was everywhere, in the peace of our village and the beauty of our landscape, but its mystery seemed to be enclosed in the tabernacle with its little lamp which glowed like the light in a creche. We crowded around our priest; we pulled at the sleeves of his surplice: "Father, hold me close, make me listen to His presence." He picked us up, one by one, and when our ears got close to the small door, slightly ajar, our hearts would beat faster. We were enraptured by our knowledge that we were listening to the heart of Love the way we listened to the vast breathing of the ocean inside a shell and to the call for love inside our families' smiles.

After Mass, we lit our candles for the procession. Perched on the shoulders of their fathers, Jeddos or big brothers, the children were up in the blue sky, enraptured with joy, songs and prayers. The mothers and the Tetas carried the infants clad in new clothes too...new souls, new brightly colored dresses, new fair, gentle sunshine for the new Spring. A new triumph of Love, dazzling, sovereign, infinite like all the hands which turned up their palms in a gesture of offering and greeting.

Under our bomb-strewn sky, they still go on, these processions, in long lines of refugees, in long lines of families in mourning. The fathers and the Jeddos hold the candles and their shoulders are slumped under the throbbing memory of the gentle weight of their children. The mothers and the Tetas walk with their arms cradled around an aching emptiness. The children pray, their hearts broken by broken loves.

But Love is still singing and, above the bloody, smokey ruins, banners are raised in the gentle breeze: "Lord, forgive them for they know not what they do."

16

The long-feared shock hit me over the head as violently as a bombshell. It was just before the summer vacation, and some of the children were getting ready to leave.

For a long time now I had become tired of remembering, tired of alternating between hope and despair, and I would doze on my bench quietly, neither happy nor really unhappy, absent to my own self.

"Don't you want to play with us?" offered a group of children.

No, I shook my head.

"If you never play, what will you do all summer long?"

I hadn't the slightest idea and I shrugged. They asked Jad: "And you, what are you going to do? Is your father coming to pick you up tomorrow?"

"I...I can't say anything," he stammered and turned his gaze away from me.

"And Naseem?"

"Come on," Jad exclaimed impatiently, "can't you leave him alone? Tomorrow is another day."

He put his arms around my shoulders, but he kept silent. He was different. He had hardly talked to me these past few days. I felt he was worried and, at the same time, exulting. He seemed to be bonded to Sister Marie by a strange complicity. He seized every opportunity to press himself against her with total trust, and the looks that passed between them, charged with so many things which escaped me, made my heart ache. I was jealous and I could say nothing.

I didn't care if other children clung to Sister Marie's skirt. She sometimes talked to them with the soft and sunny words a mother might use and I would press my hands on my ears so as not to hear her speak. Perhaps in my deeply confused child's mind, accepting Sister Marie would have meant accepting her as a substitute for my family and thus also accepting to be shut up for life in this orphanage which, to me, could only be a jail.

But Jad! Why did he need to cling to her that way when he had such a wonderful father? It was true he was a little boy who liked everyone. With her, however, he seemed to share a secret which excluded me. This increased the numbness of my mind—as good a way as any to shield myself from more suffering.

Had I not lost my voice, I might have begun communicating with the Sisters and the other children after a while. But my inability to form any sound at all paralyzed me just as much as my grief, and I found it easier to reject everyone altogether. Besides, I was sick and tired of nodding my head up and down to say Yes, and shaking it from side to side to say No, and shrugging for everything else. Also, Jad was always by my side when I felt harassed. Once he left ...No! The closer the Summer vacation came, the more my heart and my reason refused even to think of it, and the more Jad clung to Sister Marie.

One night, during her rounds, I heard him whisper to her: "Are you sure *all* the papers are done?"

"Yes," she said.

"Sure, sure?"

"Yes, sure, sure."

"And the doctor, is he sure too?"

"Don't worry, Jad, we are going to pray a lot, both of us. Have faith!"

"You know," said Jad, "I pray every evening and every morning, and even sometimes in the courtyard and at meal time."

Was it his praying that prevented him from talking? Since he had mentioned the doctor, I assumed he was praying for a sick nun and I fell asleep reassured.

The last morning, everyone in the dormitory woke up before the birds. Ramzi was jumping up and down on his bed and singing at the top of his voice: "It's vacation time! Tonight, can you believe it, I'll be sleeping next to my Mama!"

Vacation time. Did that have a meaning any longer, with the war? Did it mean vacations in a cage for those of us who couldn't leave? Was Jad going to stay? Had his father found a job and a room? They never talked about it. I didn't want to think about it but a creeping fear made my stomach churn. I hoped that, at least, the abominable bell would also take a break and that we wouldn't have to put up with it for a while. But, alas, as usual, it rang for breakfast.

The line was a mess. The children, especially those who were about to leave, did not bother with discipline any longer. True, the war was still there, but they were going *home*, or to what was left of it. Some of them would be going into refugee camps, but tonight, blessed happiness, they would sleep close to their loved ones.

I went out into the yard where the tree stretched its wonderful foliage. Allah, how beautiful it was! I clung to it as if it were human. Could it tell they were *my* hands stroking it? How could it bloom all alone, without landscapes, without the singsong of springs, without lizards, beetles, katydids or grasshoppers, without bunches of ferns and heather? Were the sun and the birds enough to make it happy?

I walked up to Jad who was sitting on our bench. He was swinging his legs, visibly worried. I wanted to write on a piece of paper: "Jad, is your father coming today?" I suddenly realized that my whole life was hanging on that single question. But I couldn't bring myself to express it. I was too afraid of what the answer might be. No, it was better not to think.

He was called to the parlor. I was overcome by such panic

that I didn't even notice that he didn't ask me to follow him as he had the other times. Ramzi took his place at once.

"I saw Jad's father when I passed through the upper schoolyard," he said. "Looks to me as if he is coming to pick him up."

He was watching me with kindness, undoubtedly perplexed to find me alone.

"Don't worry," he said, "he will come back."

I dashed to the dormitory and opened his nightstand. Empty! I turned over his pillow. His mother's prayerbook had disappeared! I felt a terrible emptiness where my heart should have been. I sank to the tiled floor and rolled on it, tormented by an indescribable pain. Sister Marie tried to catch me. I hadn't seen her come in. I fought her so savagely that she had to let go of me. Despair was fast engulfing me and I began to choke.

Then I screamed. My scream filled up my mouth and my ears and flowed out of me like burning lava. It drowned the dormitory, the orphanage, the whole earth.

Did it reach all the way out to her in heaven, this scream which was dedicated to her—my mother, my life, my breath, my death?

I screamed until my strength was exhausted, but not my pain. The ensuing silence frightened me. It sounded like the silence in my village after death had swept through.

I stared at the door. Jad would never again push it open to exclaim: "Quick! Come on, hurry up. *He* is waiting for us!" He had taken his voice away along with his book, his picture, his miniature car, his soccer ball and his magic "will come." And his laughter! Allah, how empty the dormitory was without it. Allah, how dark and empty!

I kept staring at the door. Suddenly I saw it being pushed open—not impatiently but cautiously, slowly, as though by someone who didn't want to get caught. Jad's head appeared, hesitant, then he came forward with an odd step.

There was a solemnity in him that I had never seen before. My heart stopped beating and then started again, pounding erratically. He was here, in front of me, and I couldn't believe my eyes.

Had I unwittingly fallen asleep? Was I dreaming about him? I did often see my family in a very clear dream. Ramzi said that when the dead appear to you like that, it means they are coming to get you. I was not afraid, though. Only nightmares and the ghosts who regularly came by my bed could frighten me.

I called timidly, "Jad, is that you?"

I can't describe the look on his face when he heard the sound of my voice. He froze in disbelief, then twirled around singing: "Oh, Mother, oh, Mama, it worked. It worked!"

Sister Marie had not dared to intervene yet. He went to shake her sleeve: "Did you hear that? He talks! He talks! He talks! Please, Sister, can you go tell my Papa? Because I must tell Naseem, I must tell him...you know what."

She kissed Jad and stroked my hair. But her hand was still foreign to me. When one believes for too long that one is alone, one ends up unable to know other people's hearts.

I was exhausted by so many emotions and just as stupefied as Jad by the return of my voice. And, just as my father had once upon a time lost the North, the South, the East, and the West, so did I. I no longer wanted to understand anything. All this upset my soul too deeply. I don't know why I thought of my drawing and almost asked Jad if he would take it along. This thought revived my grief, but this time, instead of screaming, I began to cry.

Jad sat down on the floor next to me and announced solemnly: "I am going to tell you something and you'll stop crying. Guess what, Naseem. My Papa is taking both of us away forever."

"Both of us away forever?"

It took a very long time for me to understand. Great joys

are like great pains. When they suddenly hit you, you may hear the words but their meaning does not sink in at first. You repeat them as an echo. Then, slowly, something gets tied or untied inside you and then... My heart opened. The earth opened. The whole universe became the chime of Easter bells, became Christmas carols, became the sun.

My father, my mother, at long last I found your living faces again and the love you had nurtured within me came back to life. Allah, how I longed to live! Forever. Even though the war had taught me that "forever" might die in a split second. But "forever" didn't matter any longer. Each second immersed in love became eternal. I was confusedly aware of this. Yet, through the fairy-tale happiness that submerged me while the war kept on rumbling outside, I knew deep inside of me, and forever, that I wanted to be life, all life—open-hearted, open-handed, like my mother, like my father, like my village, like Jad and his wonderful father. My hand would sow and reap life...yes, even through the war.

I looked at Jad. He seemed disappointed and sad: "Do you care so little that instead of jumping with joy, you keep right on crying? It's not fair! Can't you understand that we've become real brothers forever?"

Oh Jad, Jad, my true, wonderful little brother! I was too overcome by joy to be able to put it into words. I still needed a little time for my heart to finish thawing. If only you could know how much I needed you, your gentle and kind ways, so true and spontaneous, your chit-chat, your impatience, your "Quick, hurry up!" and your "Oh, St. Elijah, what have I done to you that you sent me such an idiot to put up with!" How I needed all of you to escape the treacherous bogs of the roads to nowhere and find my way again onto the paths of life.

Yes, I was crying. But the serene glitter of my tears was like a smile. Tears like a prayer. Tears dedicated to my parents, to God, to your father (now *my* father on this earth, may Allah keep him forever above our heads and fill him with peace and love!), and to you, Jad, little boy with a mother's heart who had given me so much.

I was crying and I stammered out: "Jad, my brother for real?"

And you, impatient again, yourself again, little squirrel who sowed tenderness, you leapt to your feet and pulled my arm: "I'm telling you, for goodness sake! Oh, St. Elijah, what have I done to you that you sent me such an idiot to put up with! Quick, come on, hurry up. *He is waiting for us!*"